FIGHT FOR THE LIFE

URII ORLOV

Fight For The Life
by Urii Orlov

ISBN 978-1-7776054-1-4

All images, layout, and design by Jaimen Shires unless otherwise credited.

Printed in Canada
Published by Canadian Allied Services

Special Thanks To:

My mother Natalia, who helped me write this book in Russian language first. You help me grow by stretching myself to look at the past and find beauty in troubled times. The universe wants to help us.

Rose Hong, who is stuck in a foreign country and cannot come here. Even as far away as she is, Rose helped me write this book. When I was too tired to write, I recorded my words and she sent them back to me all written out. You made my life so much better, and I am very grateful to have you in it.

The stories in this book are true, but I changed a few details to protect people from harm. Even with different names, the truth is here, and I hope you are able to understand the message that life is beautiful, the future is bright and all that happens to us is meant for good in the end.

FIGHT FOR THE LIFE

URII ORLOV

"My lovely son and darling wife, I made a lot of mistakes in my life. I was a bad person, I killed and injured many people but thank God I realized that I was wrong, and I finally became a good person. I helped many people who had the same lifestyle that I got before, and they left the criminal world because of my advice. This person who just shot me had only two choices, to kill you, my son and you, my wife Olga, or kill me. I chose for them to kill me. I was very deep in the criminal world and I knew that I would one day need to pay for leaving there. Now I am talking to you my son, please do not make the same mistake that I did many years ago when I killed those guys who killed my father. Do you see what happened to me? Prisons, violence, and now I am laying down alone on the ground in a pool of blood, and I won't see you growing up. I won't be able to see and play with your kids when they are born. Please don't be mad at the guy for killing me. He had a job to do so forgive this person and let go. The only way to protect the family is to move on and make a good life for you and your mother. I love you both! Now I have to go, I hear my parents calling me..."

- Oleg

CHAPTER ONE

THE FIGHT TO LIVE

I was born on October 8th, 1982, in Odessa, Ukraine. But honestly, I had to face my first big challenge before I was even born. Only three weeks into her pregnancy with me, my mother had decided to go to her friend who could help her to terminate the pregnancy by consuming a special drink. At the time, she did not know what else to do.

After a long talk with my father, she had understood that he was not ready to decide on whether to keep the child or not and that the responsibility would be hers to shoulder alone. My mother was very disappointed. When she arrived at her friend's house, the drink was already on the table, but she was not in a rush to take it. After spending over an hour talking about everything, her friend asked her why she had not taken the special drink. My mother did not know what to answer. She knew that she might have to take care of the baby on her own, without money and the roof over the head. "What can you give to this child?" repeated her friend.

My mother was married to her first husband at the age of nineteen, while she was a student in university, but marriage to this man did not bring her happiness. My father was not happy in his marriage either. They met when both were not free to fall in love, but the wind of changes began to blow.

When my young mother left him, she was broke and almost

living on the street. Her mother was a difficult character and often, my mother would have to leave the house to escape the terrible things that went on there. My paternal grandparents did not accept my father's decision to divorce his previous wife. Therefore, the situation of my mother was critical when she suddenly realized that she was pregnant. After a long talk with my father, she understood that he was not ready to decide on whether to keep the child or not and that the responsibility would be dumped onto the weak shoulders of my mother. My mother was very disappointed, and she did not think very deeply, so that is when she decided to go to her friend who knew how to prepare a special drink.

For one and half hours this went on, but she felt that this microscopic creation inside of her wanted to live, and she felt a need for him more than anything in the world. So unwittingly, almost mystically, I won my first fight – the fight for life - and to this day my parents are still together.

Our life was hard at that time, like most people in Ukraine, but our family was used to adversity. My grandmother, Irina, and great grandmother, Ksenia, lived in much harder times.

Many years before I was born when my great grandmother Ksenia was still young, she had been hiding in the basement cellar - cold, alone, and scared - for three days, with no heat and no light. She was terrified to go outside because her mother had told her that Tzar Nikolai II, and his family had all been assassinated a few days ago. She realized now that not all aristocrats were protected, and that her family could be killed at any time. Ksenia was a beautiful young lady, who was well educated, like all aristocrats in Russia. She spoke five languages and could play every classical instrument that was ever made. She was cultured and even though she now lived in poverty, she still held herself with poise and grace. Ksenia and her daughter Maria hid in their beautiful palace, burning their precious antique furniture just to stay warm.

One afternoon Ksenia was sitting in the living room sipping a cup of tea, remembering the old days when life was good and she was surrounded by wealth. The maids, who were like the family, were washing the clothes in the laundry. Suddenly, she heard men's voices in the yard singing revolutionary songs. She could tell that they were drunk. Ksenia told her daughter Irina to run, quickly as she could, and hide in the root cellar. Irina ran to the basement, lifted up the dusty old rug and climbed down into the dark, hidden root cellar in the floor. Her maid straightened the rug back in place over the cellar door and moved a table on top of it to distract the intruders. She pretended to be cleaning the room when the men arrived. They never found her because Ksenia had been through this before and knew her life depended on being as quiet as a mouse. When they looked in the basement, she hardly took a breath until they were gone.

Ksenia was very fortunate that she had heard the revolutionaries in the yard, because that gave her the few precious seconds she needed to gather up all of her jewellery and hide it in a bowl in the sink, with the dirty laundry. The maids lazily washed the clothes as if nothing was wrong.

The men came in and tore the entire house apart, looking for any money or gold they could find. Within two hours they left with everything they could carry. As they left, one of the men walked up and punched Ksenia's mother in the face so hard that she fell down on the floor. Another guy told them that in two days Ksenia's family would have to evacuate the house, because now all their goods belonged to the revolutionary party.

My family quickly packed up what they could and my great grandmother gave some of her jewellery to the staff so that they could escape the tyranny. With such notice she was not able to secure a place on the ships that went to Europe or the USA, so she chose to travel to Azerbaijan because many aristocrats had fled there.

The jewellery helped them travel from Saint Petersburg to Baku, the capital of Azerbaijan. The journey was a difficult one. When I asked my grandmother about the trip she said, "Bad things happened." She would say nothing more. The roads were not safe for women travelling and it is a miracle that they arrived at all.

With all of the jewellery that they had hidden, she could have bought a new palace, but by the time the bribes were all paid, there was only enough money to buy a small apartment with no bathroom. This is where eventually, my mother was born.

Ksenia was my great-grandmother. Her aristocratic family was very wealthy and had over one-hundred and fifty household staff. She had gone to finishing school in Paris and her family owned houses in Switzerland and a number of other countries in Europe. In the palace in Saint Petersburg where Ksenia was born, there were over two-hundred rooms. However, when they fled to Azerbaijan, their apartment was only one small room and a kitchen. The washroom was an outhouse in the backyard, and it was shared with all the tenants in the building. There were over three-hundred neighbours in the building. It was a terrible step down from the life she had lived at the palace, but she treated everyone she met with love, and lived her meagre life with her head held high.

She was a wonderful lady, and everyone loved her. They were very poor... so poor that her friends and neighbours took turns bringing her food to help the family survive. She was an excellent seamstress and to thank them for the food they brought for her family, she sewed clothing for their children.

My Grandmother Irina worked for the government but had a very small salary. On New Year's Eve she always invited her co-workers over and had put out chocolates as a special treat for them. The first time she did this my mother, who had never seen chocolates in her life, gobbled them all down because she was sure she would never see them again. My mother loved to play the piano and many other instruments as well, so music often filled their tiny home. My mother would lay on the bed and play the violin, while Ksenia cooked for her. She told her grandma that the teacher said she would get better results from playing the violin laying down. I don't think her grandma believed her, but she didn't say anything about it because at the very least, she was practising.

My great-grandmother was a very intelligent woman. Although she was born into wealth and privilege, she died at the age of 90, broke, selling sunflower seeds near the Orthodox church to keep food on the table. She could not talk to anybody about her aristocratic background, because she was so scared that the KGB would put her in jail or kill her because of her heritage. My great-grandmother had been fluent in 5 foreign languages and played particularly well on the piano and violin. She could have taught foreign languages or given piano lessons but because of fear of being jailed by government forces, she hid her talents to avoid having to answer any questions that might get her into trouble.

That is where I came from, a life of big wealth and also big poverty.

I grew up in a four-room apartment with my family. I remember this apartment like it was today: The old wooden entrance door, painted a deep red; the five bells on the wall with a handwritten name above or below each of them. Most of the bells did not work, so visitors knocked very hard on the door or yelled the name of the person they were visiting. When you came inside, you saw a long narrow corridor. Along the corridor, there were many trunks and boxes. There were no lights in this hallway and people always tripped over the boxes. The walls were dirty, with old paint peeling from them. The wooden floor was in very poor shape and when people walked, I could hear a loud wheezing. It was very hot and always smelled bad from cooked fish or soup with beef bones.

I can not explain why but I miss this place. A different family lived in each bedroom, and there were many violent secrets. In one room a man was beating his wife, and in another a man was drinking, getting louder and more angry, the more he drank. There were many terrible things happening all around me but we spent all the holidays together, nobody was alone, people would hate each other for the moment when they were fighting but love each other at the same time. That's how it felt.

In our apartment lived one guy with his wife. He lost his leg in the second world war and had an artificial leg that was made from wood. I remember him, he was always drunk. Anyway, there was one bathroom which was shared between all families. After his visits to the washroom, he would forget to turn the light off. Everyone asked him many times to turn off the light but he always seemed to forget. Maybe he did it on purpose, I don't know.

All the other families had a meeting in the kitchen and after drinking a few bottles of vodka they decided to educate the old guy. They waited for him to go to the washroom and after he forgot to turn the light off, they started to beat him. The old dude was a strong guy and to protect himself he took his wooden leg and he used it to fight his neighbors. He hit a few of the men on the head. There was a lot of blood in the kitchen. After about half an hour, the police arrived along with an ambulance, but the funny thing was that nobody could find the wooden leg. We all looked everywhere but it was gone. Finally, we found out that the neighbor's dog had taken the leg and hid it. After the leg was found, everyone was laughing and of course drinking vodka. They asked forgiveness from each other, kissed each other, and sang songs until early morning! So, there were some good times among the bad and happy memories between the violence and anger.

My father was violent to me as well, so violence became all I knew when I was younger. I would get hit and beaten if I didn't make good marks in school. I got smart about the beatings and one day when he grabbed a stick to beat me with, I said I was too cold and wanted more clothes. I came outside with many layers on. He beat me, but it hurt a lot less with extra clothing on.

The clothes I would wear were not the proper clothing to go to school and that embarrassed me. We were so poor that during graduation in secondary school, I was the only boy who did not have a suit to wear on prom night. I now know how psychologically difficult it was for my parents to not afford to buy the essential things I needed. It was a constant struggle to keep food on the table, and some nights we had nothing to eat. We would go to sleep with our stomachs growling with hunger. At times I had to steal food and money just to survive. Other kids were richer than me and I felt bad that I stole from them, but I wanted to eat.

I sometimes wonder if this was how my self-hatred started. I wanted to control everything in my life: my present, my future, and my child's future, which was absolutely wrong. As humans, we cannot control these things.

CHAPTER TWO

THE FIGHT TO LEARN

Once, at the age of five, I was watching a movie about Kung-Fu with Bruce Lee. I was so impressed that I decided to train and become as powerful as Bruce Lee. I made a goal for myself to be able to do five hundred push-ups at a time. I made up a training schedule - two times a day, seven times a week - and have never missed a training session yet. This was the beginning of my fascination with the martial arts and was a healthy channel for my crazy energy. It was a difficult time for my mother, because she was worried that I trained too much.

After two years of training, I had nearly reached my goal. I could do four hundred push-ups at a time. It was around this time that I started to train in the Chinese martial art of Wushu. Because I was strict with myself from a very young age, I did very well at Wushu and won many, many tournaments. I ended up developing a reputation as a tough gymnast and competitor.

Wushu has a deep, secret meaning. First, it is a philosophy that involves taking a deep look at the world around us. The hidden symbols manifest themselves in the gymnastics positions. While practicing Wushu, you must overcome all external difficulties to find knowledge inside yourself. Some of these movements signify natural forces, such as typhoons, while others represent qualities like progress, success, or collapse. Many movements are also related to a particular animal's behaviour. All movements in Wushu are performed in certain rhythms that symbolize integrity and infinity. Wushu develops your own internal supernatural power. Some Wushu Masters can light a fire without matches or even break the rocks without touching them and many other wild things like that. I have seen it with my own eyes.

You cannot practice Wushu if you are not comfortable in your own skin. If you do, you will have problems like mental and psychological blocks that I ran into, because energy moves strongly while practicing Wushu. If you are not accepting of yourself the energy can get stuck and the blockage can cause damage to your body. I understood this through my training but did not know how it could affect my life in other ways.

Negative thoughts about myself started to grow inside of me, and by the time I was eleven, I had become friends with boys that were ten to fifteen years older than me. They trained in English boxing and mixed martial arts. They told me that Wushu was not a good sport for a man. They said it was a dance not a sport. They said only boxing is for real men. Because of their influence, I started to hate the sport that I had spent all my life training in and in which I was successful.

Schoolteachers did not like me, classmates feared me, and I did not have a good relationship with my parents. The only place I felt successful and respected was in sports. However, I started to question if Wushu was really the right sport for me, and not just because the older boys said so. I criticized myself constantly and did not accept myself as I was. I always found fault with everything I was doing or how I was doing it. I thought if I did that I would be accepted and liked by others. It was like there was a third person who constantly watched how I was walking, how I was talking to people, what I was wearing. Every plan had to satisfy this imaginary third person. I basically evaluate everything on me from the outside, and my evaluation was based on fear of what others would say and think about me.

Ah, but my new friends had expensive cars and beautiful women! I knew they were criminals because you couldn't make a lot of money from sports at that time, so you had to do something to support your sports. I started hanging out with them because I thought those guys were perfect. In a time when most people in the country did not have money for food, they didn't look troubled or worried. I became a close friend with one guy from their team named Sergei. He was the one who finally convinced me to quit Wushu and start to do boxing.

I trained in boxing for a few months, and I liked to be in the ring. I liked punching bags. It was the best outlet for my violent anger and pain. I was good at it and placed second in regional competitions in boxing.

Although I had good results, I did not feel very good. I felt that there was something wrong with me. I was psychologically broken down for some reason. One of my coaches took me aside and convinced me to go back to Wushu, so I did. I stopped boxing and came back to my old sport. However, I did not stop the relationship with my older friends. Their influence on me was huge. I wanted to be just like them: I imitated the way they were walking, talking, their vision, their points of view and sense of life. Gradually, by imitating them I slowly stopped being myself.

It was around this time when I met Oleg.

I was around eleven or twelve years old, and he was nineteen when he came to visit from Russia. He stayed with us for only one day and then left, back to Russia. We spent all night talking. By this time, he told me he had already done his second or third time in jail.

Oleg was a young boy who grew up in a small town in Siberia. He was only one year old when his father was killed. His father was a very honest and fair policeman who was murdered because criminals wanted to buy him out, but he would not take any money or bribes from them. His parents had lived in an apartment building on the eleventh floor and the killers made him jump out of the window. They wanted it to look like suicide.

Since his father had been killed and his mother worked all the time just to keep food on the table, it was a very hard life. Even though she worked all the time, sometimes, they still didn't have anything to eat. He almost never went to school and his mother could not do anything about it. From a very early age, he began boxing and became a boxing champion in his town. He grew up to be a strong, tall boy. He never made it very far because he wanted to eat, and amateur boxing does not bring any food on the table, especially at that time. He told me that boxing gave him power and the knowledge of how to fight but not much else.

When Oleg was older, he found out what exactly happened to his father on that fateful day. Three policemen who were his father's colleagues came to his apartment. They sat down in the kitchen and one-year-old Oleg was sleeping in the next room. His colleagues told Oleg's father that he went too far, and he must die. They promised him that if he jumped by himself, they won't touch his son. He chose to jump. Before leaving the apartment, one of the policemen said that he wants to see the baby. They went in his room and saw Oleg sleeping. The same guy who wanted to see the baby told his associates that his feelings were saying to him that this child will give them problems when he grows up and it is better to kill him. They reminded him that it is bad luck to touch a child. Especially if they promised his father before he passed away. Anyway, they vowed that this child would never know what exactly happened on this day. They kept the truth hidden for many years, but they did not know that revenge was going to still find them.

Even thirteen years after his death, Oleg's father was a very respected officer and well known in the police world. His friends and colleagues promised Oleg's mother that they would find the guys who killed her husband. When Oleg was fourteen years old, the three ex-policemen were found guilty of the murder of Oleg's father. This devastated Oleg, and he decided to be in the courtroom with a gun. He waited for the perfect moment, when the guards were busy and not keeping a close eye on the three thugs. He walked up to them quickly and shot all three of them. He killed two of them, but one was only badly injured and managed to live. This disappointed Oleg, but years later he would meet the man in jail and slit his throat.

Violence was how Oleg solved problems. His mother passed away from overworking when he was sixteen. Oleg quit boxing and became friends with a few criminals who had been in jail in the past. He thought he wanted to work with them. He and his friends would ask small or medium businesses for money in exchange for protection. They hit up restaurants, gas stations, and people who were selling clothes or vegetables in the street markets. Basically, the businesspeople hired criminals to protect them from other criminals, but of course, they were obligated to hire them. At that time, there were many organizations like that.

All the organizations eventually diversified and split off from each other and went by the nickname or name of its leader. Oleg's syndicate nickname was Savage. For example, if somebody came to one businessman but this guy had already hired Savage's organization, the businessman would say to them, "Savage protects me," then they would call Savage and ask him if it is true. If it was, then they would go looking for other victims to protect. If some businessman would say, "I do not need any protection," the minimum the criminals would do was to set fire to the business, or they might kill him or his family members. You know, just to make a point.

Of course, there was a lot of competition between the criminal organizations and there were many gang wars between them for the territory. During the 90s, almost all factories in the ex-USSR stopped working and many people lost their jobs. However, the people were able to travel to Turkey, Poland, or other countries to buy clothing or used cars which they could bring back to sell. During that time anybody could leave their poverty-stricken area and travel to a first world country so almost everybody did business of some kind. Of course, the strong guys started to build the organization to protect the new businessmen, but in real life they just wanted to take a percentage from their sales. The police were paid off by criminals and those policemen who did not accept the bribe money were simply killed. The government did not care about what was going on. The politician's goal was to skim off as much money as they could and send it offshore, then leave the country as soon as possible.

All this, Oleg told me that night. I learned a lot from the talk with him, and he gave me a lot of examples of why to not become a criminal and to do everything right in life. He told me, "All criminals are stupid because they are fighting against the system, but the government always wins because in the end the government is the biggest criminal. Better to have normal work, and a family. There is no good life from crime, Urii."

Oleg admitted to me that his life was fucked up but that he was going to do everything possible to change it. It was a very important conversation for me, and I realized for sure that I do not want to be a criminal. From the outside it may look like they have a nice life but it's only from the outside. He left me with many things to think about but I was not quite ready to change my own ways.

CHAPTER THREE

THE FIGHT TO WIN

When I was back in Wushu training, I started to train a lot, because I was preparing for a national competition, but I felt that my psychological state was not healthy. From the outside everything was fine, but on the inside I felt that I was losing the ground under my feet. Also, I had another problem: I was in a rush. I wanted to be the champion of the world and I wanted to do that very quickly. So I trained hard to prepare for the national championships. I wanted to be the champion, no matter what. I was so focused on the future and didn't want to live in the now but the problem was that I hated who I was. I did not accept my past and present, so much that I only wanted to focus on the future. I was in a rush. I couldn't even walk slowly. I wanted to have everything very quickly. I was afraid that if I had to wait, it would be too late. I trained extra hard. I was on a mission to be the perfect Wushu gymnast and I worked tirelessly, always correcting my form. I was very self-critical because I thought it would make me into the best gymnast.

One day, our coach had me do an interesting exercise. He tied my legs and hands behind my back and pushed me in a swimming pool four meters deep. The goal was to stay in the water for three minutes with tied legs and hands. For the first eleven attempts I fell to the bottom of the pool and had to be rescued by my coach. My problem was that I panicked and tried to survive, and as a result I lost a lot of energy very quickly and almost drowned. On my twelfth attempt, I just stopped and accepted my situation. I was relaxed and peaceful in my heart. My body went down to the bottom of the swimming pool and naturally, without thinking, I pushed off the bottom of the swimming pool with my legs and I came to the surface of the water. I had a few seconds to take some air in and repeated the exercise.

After five times through this exercise I was exhausted and figured out that I might spend one minute but that left two more minutes before I finished this training. A new solution came by itself. Once again, I pushed off the bottom and when I took air in my lungs, I realized that my body could stay on the surface of the water if I was relaxed and calm inside. Of course, it's exceedingly difficult when you are tired, and your hands and legs are tied. It was hard to keep my balance, because sometimes my back was up, and my face was down in the water. The main thing was to remain calm inside, not panic and try to relax as much as I could. I know for sure that I will remember those two minutes for the rest of my life.

The most important lesson I learned from this exercise is to accept your situation, whether it's good, difficult, easy, pleasant, or unpleasant it does not matter. Trust that the universe will eventually bring you the right solution.

Today I realize that I was so overly hard on myself and tried to control everything about myself which made me feel insecure and even worse at everything I did.

This reminds me of my school in Odessa. On the first floor, there were big mirrors on the wall and in the afternoon, everybody had to walk past them to go to the cafeteria. Every time I passed the big mirrors, I watched myself in the mirror. I did not like the way I walked. For some reason, I did not like the length of my stride. I thought maybe my steps were too long. Every time I passed the mirrors, I found something new that I did not like in how I walked. I started trying different ways to move my feet while I was walking. Every day before I left my home, I practiced in front of the mirror how I should walk when I go out. But of course, when I was out, I would forget and because of that I was always mad at myself. I did not accept myself for who I was. My critical mind was turning on me and I was ashamed of myself. I began to hate who I was.

I studied poorly in school until the age of thirteen. School was not interesting to me and I thought it was not important. I did not go to school often but if I went, I got in trouble. I often was a visitor to the principal's office. The school where I studied was one of the most dangerous in the city. It was filled with drug addicts, criminals, and lots of violence. There were thugs beating people up in the washroom every day. You weren't safe there. In the whole city, only our school was the only one that had security guards.

One time, when my mother went to school for a parents meeting, she told my father after that all the parents were saying that they were scared to send their kids to school because of me. I was real trouble. I invited into my group the worst students from school and neighborhood, and we organized like a mini criminal organization. We extorted the money from students at our school and even other schools next to ours. No one could do anything. We were not even scared of the police because they could not jail us. We were too young.

Our physical education teacher came to school drunk this

one time and during the class one girl could not do the exercises properly. The teacher gave her a slap in the face. She cried a lot, so we found out where this teacher was living and we waited for him in the evening next to his house. We attacked him from the back and beat him violently. Everyone in school had an idea of who beat him, but the people were too scared to talk.

We were like the kings, until one day we got a new teacher in our school. We heard that this dude was fucked up in his head and he killed a teenager in the juvenile correctional facility where he used to work. After this incident, he lost his job, and he was sent to our school to teach. Also, we heard that he was in the war in Afghanistan and he tortured Afghan soldiers who had been captured. When he arrived in our school, we became less wild but still we did bad stuff sometimes. I will never forget this one day when in the washroom we took the money from one boy. He was a strong teenager. When we asked him to give us his money, he tried to run away but a strong kick in the solar plexus knocked him to the ground and we took his purse. The next day our educational teacher asked me to come to his office. As soon as I crossed the threshold, he kneed me in the stomach and beat me violently for a few minutes. Even my father did not beat me so badly. Before leaving his office, he said to me, "If you touch my son again, I will cut your head off." I could tell he was serious and would kill me if we tried anything again with his son.

After this incident, I honestly planned to kill this dude. I followed him for a few days to find out where he is living and where he is going normally. One day I saw him pick up his ten-year-old son from the school for disabled kids. I learned that his youngest son had cerebral palsy. I was very surprised when I saw him be so kind with his son. He was kissing him, playing with him, he cleaned his mouth from the drool. I was really impressed! I had never expected that that crazy motherfucker could be so kind with a sick child. Later, I also found out that his wife passed away in a car accident and he alone took care of his two sons. This situation made me change my mind and I told all my friends to not touch this guy anymore.

I was so impressed by this situation. That was the first time I really started to think about my own life. I felt sorry for his sick kid and at the same time I was jealous because my father has never been so kind like this man. Deep in my mind I wished to have a father like this teacher. After this situation with this crazy teacher I was less violent in school, but teachers and students were still scared of me.

Finally, I came to school in the morning and I saw one of my teachers and the principal at the entrance door. They did not let me enter the school. The principal told me that all the teachers were ready to give me good marks on the condition that I never come back to the school. I wasn't sure how to take that. I guess that I was so violent that they would do anything to get rid of me! The teachers may have said they didn't want my violent attitude at the school, but I also didn't hear of anyone else getting offered good grades to just go away in the entire history of the school!

Before this age, I almost did not study in school. In my life I had only sports. Only in the gym did I feel comfortable. Even training camp before competition brought me happiness. For sure, I was very tired, even exhausted, but my passion was stronger than the physical endurance of my body. My mind drove my body. When I did sports I had a feeling that I was in seventh heaven, but when I wasn't training I did not know what to do. I felt lost. I did not have much respect for my teachers, and I was also not very close with my parents.

When I was fourteen years old, my father beat my mother very badly and I realized that I had to stand up to him to protect her or she might not live long enough to see me grow up.

One day, before I had opened the entrance door of our apartment could already hear the voice of my father yelling, "You fucking bitch, I kill you right fucking now!" and then I heard my mother's voice, "Please no! Please no!" I had already told my father a few weeks ago when he tried to beat my mother, "If you touch my mother again, I am going to kill you!" He knew that I was not joking. He beat her so many times, I cannot even count on two hands. I remember even when I was a baby how angry and violent he was with her. It was burned in my mind and I will remember that forever but now that I had grown up, my duty was to protect my mother.

I quickly opened the door and rushed to the living room. I saw my mother lying down on the floor and my father beating her with a stick. I came at him from the back and caught his hand by the stick. I was scared crazy, but I knew it was my duty to protect my mother. I took the stick from his hand and pushed him hard. He fell on the floor and I swung the stick at him, ready to crush the life out of him but my mother knelt down in between me and my father and said, "Please do not do it, he gave you life." I looked at her in anger, not wanting to stop, but something in her eye stopped me and I threw the stick on the floor in disgust. It was the last time he ever beat her. I think he knew if he did, he would not breathe again after I was finished with him. I had lost all respect for my father at the time.

The only people I respected were my coaches. In Wushu that year, I ranked second in regionals and third in international tournaments. Training was my life. It was all that mattered to me. But one day when I was training, I started to feel pain in the hip area of my right leg. I thought that I had somehow pulled a muscle. In the sports world it's quite a normal situation. That winter evening when I was going back home, I was very exhausted from my training. It felt like I was starting to get the flu. Halfway to my house, I sat down on a fallen tree and suddenly I felt tired like an old man. I got a feeling that something bad was happening. I was worried. I even had thoughts that maybe I did not want to live anymore.

The next day when I woke up and got out of bed, I felt a fever. Suddenly, I had the pain in my hip again. I tried to make a Wushu position but because of the harsh pain in the hip I couldn't do it. I tried to ignore the severe pain during training that day but again I couldn't. It was a crippling pain and I had to stop. The reality that I wasn't able to practice Wushu anymore was too hard to accept. I took a pause in training and hoped that the pain would go away but it didn't. I even participated in a competition but I did poorly because I was in constant pain.

My rivals from other cities were incredibly surprised to see me do so poorly but I didn't want to explain to anybody what was going on with my health. It was difficult to accept that I was finished with sports forever. It was my life, my air, and my sole purpose for being. I spent more time in the gym than I did anywhere else. I did not know if there was a life outside the gym because I had no other interests.

The goals I had for my life suddenly disappeared. My guiding star had faded away. I continued to go to the gym but it was not the same anymore. I could not use my legs. I already knew that for me, competitive sports were now in my past and I felt that others knew that too, but nobody wanted to say it to me. Slowly, I started to show signs of depression. I did not talk to anybody. I visited the doctors but no one could tell me what was wrong. However, one summer day, I went with my mother to an orthopedic surgeon and he finally gave me the right diagnosis, Perthes Disease. Based on what I found on the internet, Perthes is, '...a childhood condition that affects the hip when blood supply to the rounded head of the thigh bone is disrupted. Without adequate blood supply, the bone cells die.'

When I first got my diagnosis, I was really shocked. The doctor told me that I was in a late stage of the illness. Although he did not tell me this, I am absolutely certain that the illness started from my deeply rooted self-hate. In my opinion, the true cause was deeply related to my subconscious, my relationship with the world, and how I see myself as part of this world. I do not know why, but I completely forgot the things I had learned through Wushu once I got this disease. I was scared and depressed. I hated who I was, so I looked for someone to be like. I saw my friend with a bad leg and I started to emulate how he was walking. I felt forced to make big changes in my life and was not happy to move forward. I had nothing to move forward to and didn't like who I was, so I took on his injury in my mind.

My mother was sympathetic toward my situation. She understood the feelings. She always liked literature, books, and arts, and helped me to change my priorities in life. She convinced me that there are many other interesting things in life, and I could set other goals, I just need to be open to looking at that.

I almost stopped going out at all, and I did not communicate with anybody or only said the basic stuff like hello and goodbye. I limped a lot and was embarrassed of myself. When I was walking, sometimes I did not have any pain but I still found myself limping! On a subconscious level I felt like a flawed person. I wanted to be sorry for myself and I wanted other people to feel sorry for me too.

I was beating myself up and the rush of anger inside of me transformed on a physical level. I wanted to get everything very quickly, but I did not live up to my own expectations, and so, I hated myself. I only accepted myself if I succeeded in the future. But this future I had set out for myself was not realistic, and when I did not meet expectations, I wanted to kill myself.

Everywhere at home or outside, I controlled every step that I made while walking.

Only a few times over the last twenty-four years have I forgotten about my leg while I was walking. Normally, my mind would be constantly focused on my leg. When I walk now, I don't limp but sometimes I still have the pain. Also, I have the pain in my thigh area when I try to touch the knee of my right leg to my chest. A few times in the last twenty-four years I did not control my walk while walking, I touched the chest with the right knee and I did not have pain.

The pain and flexibility of the hip joint is related to the way I am walking. If I am relaxed and do not pay attention to my walk - basically walk without controlling my walk - I am perfectly okay. But it is the hardest thing to achieve!

I think that my illogical control of my walk relates to my childhood self-esteem problems. It was really about the difficulty that I had to accept myself as I was. If you talk to me in person, you might think that I am the most confident person in the world, but that is only on the surface. One year later, I went to the doctor for the checkup and he told me that my disease was getting worse. He mentioned that I might always limp or even not be able to put weight on my leg.

The doctor recommended that I put the leg in a cast for one year. The cast would go all the way up my leg until the abdomen and I would have to keep it on for an entire year. My mother knew my character and she saw my psychological state. She told me not to accept the doctor's advice. I think I was so depressed at the time that if I had been put in that cast I would have stayed in bed for that whole year. If I did that, I would be even more depressed and who knows how it would have ended...

Instead, I used crutches for a few months and I promised my mother that I would change my attitude towards my situation. I am very thankful for my mom's help in changing my attitude.

Basically, from that one conversation, I redirected my goal-oriented character toward education. In the beginning studying just helped me to not think constantly about my leg problem, but later I became interested in learning. Honestly, it was exceedingly difficult to start learning everything from the beginning and I often did not sleep at night because I had to catch up on all the material that I missed.

I knew that in order to become a different person, I needed to see the world from a different angle. She told me that maybe the universe was talking to me through my illness. Maybe it was trying to send me signs. It wanted me to change something because I wasn't changing on my own. She advised me to read books, to start to study. Also, she told me, "You are going to find the truth that you did not notice before and it might be very important for your fate. If you find the right way in life, the illness will go away because you will not need it anymore."

At that moment, I felt an emptiness in my soul. I had a feeling of hopelessness, that something went out of me. All my life plans were related to sports, and sports were done for me. All my sports colleagues who I shared the happiness and sadness with, slowly forgot me. My mother started to give me simple books to read. I started with detective stories and ended up reading classic literature. I found other interests in my life: studying, reading books, and having friendships with people who are not related to sports. They had much different interests than my other friends. In the beginning it was funny for me to talk about something other than sports but I found it interesting also. I became knowledgeable in different areas of life.

Now that I could behave better, they let me go back to school. I went every day, but I was behind with all the subjects I needed. I took private classes and after school I learned a lot at home. I did not sleep during the night because I was trying to catch up on what I missed. I sometimes went to the gym but not as often as I did before.

For the first time in my life, I was not in a rush. I enjoyed life, I was living in the present and not in the future like I did before. I became less self-critical and did not feel as unhappy anymore. After a lot of hard work, I finally finished secondary school with excellent marks. The principal, who a few years ago did not allow me to enter the school, was now retired but she attended my graduation.

The principal made a speech about me and she asked me to come on stage. During the speech, I saw that the teacher who had beaten me so violently was standing at the end of the hall alone. I was happy that he was there. I heard that he quit our school, but I was sure he came to school that day to see me graduate. By the end of the ceremony, I looked for him everywhere, but I did not find him. I wanted to tell him: "Thank you!" I think that situation with this teacher laid the foundation for my change from who I was. I would say that those two negative circumstances - my bone sickness and the beating of the teacher - played a positive role in my life, because it pushed me to change.

CHAPTER FOUR

THE FIGHT TO SUCCEED

Over in Russia, Oleg had a beautiful life. He bought a few apartments, a house, even a few expensive cars. He dated many girls at the same time, until he met Olga. Olga was the opposite of Oleg, basically she was from a different world.

The way he met her is very interesting. One day, he went inside somebody's apartment. He did not rob apartments anymore but sometimes he did it just for fun. When he was inside this apartment, he realized that this family was very poor. He found only a few golden rings, no cash, and in one room he saw a wheelchair, but he was surprised when he saw lots of books. He had never seen so many books in his life. He started to read a short novel and he was so impressed by the story that he did not realize that he had spent two and half hours reading the book. He decided to leave but did not take anything from this apartment. While leaving the suite he saw a picture on the table of a beautiful, young lady. He wanted to meet her, but he figured that she was from a very different world than he was, and that she was a very different person.

For a few months he visited her apartment. For him, this place was like an escape from loud people, lies, violence, blood, prostitutes, drugs, and alcohol. He came there to read the books. He did not know why, but he wanted to meet Olga. However, he knew that it would be a really bad idea, especially for her. One time, he fell asleep while reading a book. A few hours later when he woke up, he saw that someone had covered him with a blanket, and he could hear that they were cooking in the kitchen. He wanted to jump out the window, but he remembered that the person had already seen him because he was covered with the blanket. He took his gun and tip-toed into the kitchen. He saw the girl from the picture, she was preparing a salad. He hid the gun right away and approached the table. He noticed that she was more beautiful in real life than in the picture.

As if nothing was wrong, he said, "Hi, my name is Oleg, I am sorry, I made a mistake. I went to the wrong door. It looks like we have the same lock."

"Haha, that is funny. I'm supposed to believe that?"

"Honestly, trust me, I am not a robber," said Oleg.

"I figured out already a few months ago that somebody is coming into my apartment and reading my books," she replied. Oleg was surprised that she was so bright. His first thought was that he had lost his professional chops.

"Okay, okay, alright, I came to your house to rob you but when I saw your books, I fell in love with them and the energy that your apartment has. Also, I wanted to meet you, but I was quite sure that you would not like to talk to me," said Oleg.

"Why did you think that?" asked Olga.

"Because you would see who I am," he replied.

They started to date each other and one year later they married. In the meantime, her father passed away and she did not have anybody else in her life, only Oleg. They came and visited me once. It was weird to see this couple. She was a law-abiding citizen, with a very calm temper. She did not drink alcohol and always agreed with Oleg. He was a criminal with an extremely hot temper, so hot that he would kill if he did not like something.

She knew that he was a criminal, and that he was cheating on her and he was basically the complete opposite of her. But she was in love with him and that was enough for her to keep waiting for him to show up. Sometimes she would go weeks without knowing where he was. Olga knew that when he left their apartment in the morning, she might not ever see him again.

Oleg began thinking a lot about their relationship around this time. He knew that he needed to stop the relationship with her even if he loved her because he knew that he was going to be killed one day or be put in jail for a long time. He knew it was going to break her heart when it happened, and he didn't want to hurt her. She needed to find a normal guy and settle down to a normal life. It was winter, and he came home early with a bottle of vodka. He drank half the bottle and then asked her to sit down at the table with him. Oleg looked in her eyes as he started to talk. "Olga, I love you a lot and I've never loved anybody before. You gave me a chance to know how normal people live. My world is very different from yours. I started to read books and I know now what it means to have a family. You talked to me the first time in my life about God, and I know the meaning of the word grace."

"You've opened a new world for me that I never knew about. We have an honest relationship. You love me as I am. You do not want anything from me, only me... I would like to be honest with you and tell you that I do not deserve you. I am a bad person. I do bad things to other people. I cannot have a family. If my enemies know about you and if something goes wrong, they might kill you first, that is why I cannot have children with you. I know you would be the best wife and mother in the world, but I would be the worst father in the world. Now I will leave our house and I will not come back again. You must promise me that you'll forget about me as soon as I'm gone, and you'll find a good man for you."

They both began to cry, and he hugged her close before he left the house.

CHAPTER FIVE

THE FIGHT FOR MORE

One year after being diagnosed with Perthes Disease, I went back to the doctor for a checkup and he told me that the bone destruction had stopped. Bone scar had formed, which was exceptionally good in my situation. He was incredibly surprised because I did not take any medical treatment. But unfortunately, this good news did not get rid of my old problems like inferiority complex, low self-esteem, and self-doubt. I think the negative thinking that had started before the illness took root deeply into my subconscious and I could not get rid of it. I am pretty sure that if my coach would have told me that I am good and everything is fine, maybe I would not have been so hard on myself, but he never said anything like that. My extreme level of self-critique had created a pathology. It started with being self-critical and then kept going until I started to hate myself and everything I did. I believe that our mind is a powerful tool. It can make miracles in either positive or negative ways. When we are young it's important to help children be positive, teach them to accept themselves and how they are so they can learn to love themselves. We must teach them to not be perfectionists and to know how to be happy with small things.

When I was walking and trying to tell my mind not to control my walk, a thought would suddenly appear in my head: "How will I know how to take my next steps?" and it would give me a feeling of fear. I'd start to control my walk again. It was stupid but I could not seem to do anything about it! I hated that I was unable to control the way I was thinking while I was walking. It felt silly to worry about something so simple!

Before my illness, I was always worried about competitions. Every April, we had national competitions. I was living in the future and didn't want to let my coaches down by not winning. In the nationals, I placed second in all of the Ukraine. There was only one other boy who was better than me. I was a bit better than others, but not as good as this boy. I met him and we had a pretty good relationship. We would talk during the breaks in the competition. He was from Kyiv, capital city of the Ukraine, and I found out that he trained less than me. He studied well in school and he had hobbies and friends from outside the sport. But me, I took my sports so seriously! I spent most of my time in the gym. I almost did not go to school, never did any homework, and had no friends outside the sport. I didn't even know what the word 'hobby' meant. Hobbies were not important to me because I thought they would not help me realize my goals but the results were not as good as I expected. As a result, I was more disappointed and frustrated with myself. I hated myself for failing. The fear of the future went very deep in my subconscious. That is one of the reasons why I would control my walk while walking forward. As soon as I start to walk, suddenly a little spark appears in my mind and makes me think about my leg and I start to focus on my leg. As a result, I did not let myself walk naturally, which I believe caused more problems. Those self-hating thoughts in my life happened long before the pain appeared in my right leg. With my mind controlling my leg while walking and my mind focused on the future and hating my past, I think I had unintentionally created my illness.

After secondary school, I went to medical college and successfully finished a four-year program in three years. Once I had the nurse diploma in my hands, I could start to work in the Ukraine right away or to try to find a way to go abroad. I decided to find a way to leave the country.

During my college study, I did practicums in different hospitals in Odessa. I saw how the nurses were working like dogs and making hardly any money. To survive they were doing crazy things. For example, they stole medication and sold it to patients or obliged the patients to buy it from them. It was so bad. I could not bring myself to do that, so I told myself I must find a way to get to work abroad. When I told my friends about my idea, they laughed at me, because the rich countries do not allow Ukrainian citizens to go working in their country, especially at that time, but I believed that everything would be fine.

I met a few guys who promised to help me go to the USA to work as a nurse. They took my last few dollars that I saved during the summer when I worked in the hotel as a cleaner and disappeared. I was so focused on my goal to find work that I wasn't even angry, and I wanted to leave the country so badly that I quickly started looking for another way. If I wanted to be angry with those crooks, I would not have the time to find another way. I thought, "Don't waste your energy on those guys. Focus on your goal."

After months of research to find the right people, I finally found a way to work in Germany in psychiatry. But they were looking for only one person from the Ukraine. I had three months to pass a written medical test in German. There were thousands of people who wanted this one spot! Also, I found out that other nurses started to prepare for this test one year ago and since I just found out about this possibility now, I had only three months to learn how to read, write and speak in German. I also had to learn the proper German medical terms for my work.

Everybody told me I had zero chance, and that I should not waste my time. I said to myself, "This is my only chance to get out from this poverty!" and the most important reason I wanted to try was for a chance to help my parents financially. I did not have money to hire a teacher or take German classes, so I went to the library, borrowed a lot of books, and went back to the apartment where I lived with my parents. I studied German from 7 a.m. to 5 p.m. and from 6 p.m. till 11 p.m. every day until I learned the medical terms in German. I honestly thought that my head was going to blow up. Something was strange though . . . It felt like I had already dreamed in this language before. Prior to learning this language, I had not spoken one word in German. Three months later I passed the test with the best marks out of anyone and I was the only one who was asked to go to Germany! If you saw the faces of those guys who gave me zero chance to get this job you would have laughed.

When I arrived in Germany to the place where I had to spend one year, I was honestly shocked. It was a little village in Bavaria and there was a psychiatry hospital where the patients lived permanently, but not much more. There was only one food store, the big hospital, the forest, and nothing else. But the biggest shock was when I met my supervisor for the first time. The problem was that in every village of Bavaria people speak a completely different dialect. The people from one village have difficulty understanding others from another village. He explained to me what I need to do for my job and showed me the patients that I need to take care of. After one hour talking with my supervisor, I did not understand one word of what he said or what my duties were.

Later the same day, I found out that the apartment where I would be spending one year was shared with three younger people. I had a lot of problems with them. They partied almost every night and I had to wake up at six a.m. every day to go to work. At work, most of my co-workers hated me, because in their minds I was stealing jobs from locals. It was very difficult. After a short period of time, I wanted to go back home, but I asked myself, "What am I going to do in the Ukraine? With the salary I am making here, I can help my parents and they could do the renovation in their apartment." We had lived in this apartment for fifteen years but they never did any renovations.

The first six months of life in Germany was a true hell. I was fighting with my roommates and neighbors, and three times police had to be called to stop the fights. The girls were prostitutes, and their customers caused me lots of trouble. I had to get up early and asked them to be quiet and leave. They said they would kill me if I didn't shut up and leave them alone, and that was my life every day. There was lots of yelling and problems at the apartment. Also, I had a bad relationship with my coworkers, and they tried everything they could to make me lose this job. They told lies to the chef about me. They told me they don't like immigrants because to them, we steal their jobs. They would ask me, "Why do you come and take this job? Go back to your home." They provoked me to fight and made it difficult for me to do my job. However, within a few months, I learned the right dialect from this village, and the co-workers stopped fighting with me so much.

As I got better at speaking the dialect, I also got a better relationship with my roommates. After those first six months, I met a few good people and I was not alone anymore. I even played in a theatre in the city on the weekends. I was very good at knowing how to act drunk and speak German with a Russian, Turkish or American accent. A German producer saw me and liked my performance so much he wanted to use me in other plays. It was a dream of mine to do theatre, so I enjoyed this time very much.

I remember playing the main role in a very touching performance. I played the captain. His job was to transport, on the cheap, the illegal immigrants to first-world countries. He had to bring them to a sea area that is close to the shore. Then he would give the lifeboats to the migrants and they must go by themselves to the shore. The captain always knew that these poor people had a fifty-fifty chance of survival, but he did not care so much, because his only goal was to make money. He had only one son that he had raised alone from a toddler's age. When his son grew up, he found out what kind of business his father was doing and he argued with his father all the time, he wanted him to stop. However, he did not understand that what his father did, it was everything for him, for his future. His father wanted him to study in the university, to have a beautiful house and have a beautiful wife and he knows it takes money for that.

One day, when the son argued with the captain about his business, his son was warning him if he does not stop doing this business, he is going to come to his boat and he is going to follow the illegal immigrants in the ocean. The captain did not pay attention to his words because he thought his son was scared of water and knew he could not swim.

One day, the captain got a new contract with a notice of only twenty-four hours. He was not prepared very well for this contract because of the short amount of time but he accepted it anyway. When he was in the middle of the ocean, one of his staff told him that they had only brought one lifeboat. They needed at least four, but they decided to not go back because they had already taken the money from the guy who always arranged the illegal passengers for the captain and he would be very angry if they came back with the people still on board.

The night before, the people would be dropped off, the captain had a dream. In the dream he saw his son and the son told him that he was on the boat and he was going to die because of him. He was very impressed by his dream and he took the flash lights and he went to the hold to find out if his son was really there. There were around thirty people, and everybody was asleep. He did not want to wake up the people to scare them, so he was not able to look at every face.

In the morning, while it was still dark, the immigrants were unloaded from the boat and sent to walk through the low tide, toward land. There was a thick fog and it was very hard to see. They could not tell which way the land was. The captain repeated to himself that everything was fine, his son was sleeping now and he was very intelligent and he would never do a foolish thing like that. But either way, he promised to himself that this was his last trip and that he would retire.

A few hours later when he went to his cabin, on his desk he found a letter. Right away he recognized the handwriting of his son. His son wrote to him that he was on the boat with the immigrants and he wanted to start a new life in another country alone without his father. The captain ordered them to go back to the area where they dropped off the people. When they arrived there, they only found a few dead bodies.

Another interesting play that I participated in as a main character, was where I played a big Russian criminal by the name of Anton who escaped Russia and asked for asylum in Germany. Germany accepted him and a few days later the German authorities broke into his residency and brought him to the office of a high-level security officer. The officer told him that he had not received asylum for free. They had a lot of problems with the Russian Mafia and now he would have to work for them. If not, they would send him directly back to Russia. So, he had to be in between criminals and the official authorities. But the criminals found out that Anton is working for the police and one day the criminals invite him to their meeting where they plan to kill him. Police also knew that Anton was going to be killed at that meeting but they said nothing to him. They only wanted to find enough evidence to get a reason to put the criminals in jail. And murder was very good evidence. Anton gets shot during the meeting and afterwards the police show up. This is when Anton realizes that he was only a puppet in the hands of the police. But now it was too late.

I liked these two plays very much and enjoyed playing in them. If I was not so poor at the time, perhaps I would have become a big star on stage but I had to make money to help my parents survive.

I wired all of my salary in Germany to my parents back home. With the money that I sent to them, they could buy good food and finally be able to do a nice, modern renovation to their apartment. They purchased new furniture, a TV, fridge, and everything. I was very happy to help my parents because I was thankful for them giving me life. It was a rough time in the Ukraine and my parents were struggling to survive. The economy was in a downturn and there wasn't enough money even to pay the electricity. The currency was devalued, and everyone was struggling.

To pay for my food, the room where I lived, and have some spending money, I worked under the table in the village. I did massages for old people, worked for them in the garden, I helped wherever I could. I did what I had to, to survive and it was okay for me. When I had no money to buy food, I ate whatever was left on the trays after the patients in the hospital ate dinner. My parents did not know that I was struggling to help them, but I was incredibly happy to send money because they gave me life!

I could have spent this money on myself, for example for traveling and entertainment, but I do not regret that I gave it all to my parents. I wanted them to have a good life and my struggle was not very bad. I would learn later that while my life was becoming much better, things were getting more difficult for my friend Oleg during this time.

CHAPTER SIX

THE GUNFIGHT

I had sent letters but had not heard back from Oleg during these years and was surprised to get a call from his wife, Olga. She had bad news. Problems happened after her husband had collected a debt and now he was in jail. We spoke for many hours as she explained everything that had happened. It was all terrible to hear.

Oleg had gotten a call from someone who loaned money to a woman, and she refused to pay the debt back. It was a large amount of money. Without hesitation he accepted the new contract. All his guys were busy with different files and he went alone to the woman's house. He slowly explained to her that she had no choice, and that she had to pay the money back. He took all the cash that she had in the house and all of her jewellery. He was surprised that she was so calm and did not seem to be afraid of him, which was unusual. Before leaving the house, she told him that he was going to regret taking her things. He just smirked. He had no idea that she was the mistress of the highest police boss in the city.

That same night, he had a party in his condo. His friends came to him with a few bottles of vodka and lots of food. At midnight, they were just about to call some prostitutes when they heard the doorbell ring. They knew right away that it meant trouble. They turned the music off and kept their ears open. They did not hear any steps outside, and they figured out right away that it was the police. They took out their machine guns, laid down on the floor and waited for the trouble to start.

Oleg had many condos and detached houses in the city and he slept every night in a different one. He always had with him a bunch of keys, and a few minutes before going to sleep he decided where he was going to stay overnight so no one knew exactly where he would be if they wanted to come and kill him.

He learned to sleep on his back with a gun in his right hand and AK-47 on the left side of his body. All his properties had armored doors and iron bars on the windows for protection. Also, all of them had a secret exit that even his close friends did not know about, so he could escape even if friends betrayed him.

Normally, he did not invite anybody in his place but tonight he wanted to relax with his close friends. He figured out right away that someone who was with him now had betrayed him and told the cops where he was. He had no time to think about that now though, he had to focus on the fight that was coming.

Police knew Oleg well and they figured out that his place had armored doors, armored windows, and probably secret exits too. So, if they were going to waste time breaking the entrance door the criminals were going to leave the condo through the secret exit. Police used the next-door apartment and dug out the wall adjacent to Oleg's living room. Their plan was when someone rings the bell on the door, a few minutes later the others were going to explode the wall in the next-door apartment. While at the same time, someone was going to start to break the door down with a sledgehammer and it was going to distract him for a few minutes.

For Oleg and his friends, it was not the first time that the police or other criminals wanted to get them in their living space. When the doorbell rang, they automatically took their weapons, closed the lights, and laid down close to the wall adjacent to Oleg's kitchen and not to the next-door apartment.

After the second time the doorbell rang, the wall was blown up. Oleg with his friends were seven total against a dozen policemen. The chief of police could not bring more people with him because he officially did not have the arrest warrant.

It was so noisy from the sledgehammer that was used by policemen to break the door. Three policemen started to break down the door and nine others were in the next-door apartment. Policemen did not use enough explosives for the wall made of concrete, so the size of the hole was only enough for one person to go through at time. As soon as two policemen went inside of the apartment, Oleg and his friends opened fire. A few seconds later, the police blew up almost the whole wall and a real gunfight started. A few of Oleg's friends were killed and he was seriously injured. The entrance door was almost broken through and Oleg realized that it was time to go. He did not want to bring anybody with him because one of his friends betrayed him but he did not know who. He dragged himself to the kitchen and quickly moved a cabinet away from the wall. Behind it was a secret door leading to the stairs. He used the stairs to go to the roof. On the roof, he stumbled around for a few minutes until he reached the end of the building where he found the small door. With a strong kick, he broke the door lock and used the stairs to go down, out of the building to the street. He always had a car for emergency situations waiting for him close to the secret exit.

Three of his friends were killed that night and others were seriously wounded. Very few policemen were seriously injured, but one was killed. Later Oleg found out that the police captain, who was the woman's lover, was killed in the gunfight. Oleg himself was very wounded but escaped with his life.

Oleg drove to Tatiana's house. She was one of his lovers, who lived close to him. Her house was in front of the forest. He thought if her husband was home, he would stay in the forest until morning. Especially today, he wanted her husband not to be home and yes, he was lucky, she was alone. He didn't need to explain what had happened. She already knew everything. She had heard the news that a police officer had been killed a few hours ago and now a dangerous fugitive named Oleg, nicknamed Savage, was wanted in connection with the shooting and death of the officer. Of course, his picture was shown on the news. Police knew him very well. Since the age of fourteen, he was in and out of jail. At this point, he had spent eight years behind bars.

Tatiana saw that he was bleeding a lot. She treated the wound and told him that the wound was too deep, and it wouldn't stop bleeding. She thought he might still have the bullet inside of his body. He knew if he didn't go to the hospital right away, he was going to die. But how could he get there?? The whole city was cordoned off by the police. He did not have any choice but to ask his lover to drive him to the hospital. However, he knew that if the police checked the car, they would find him, there would be another gunfight and this innocent girl might be killed. Police knew for sure what kind of car he drove and the plate number. He called his buddies, but nobody picked up the phone. He could not make up his mind whether to ask his mistress to drive him to the hospital or not.

She had known Oleg since she was very young. When Tatiana was fifteen years old, she ran away from home to live on the streets. She could not take being beaten by her stepfather anymore. To survive she started turning tricks even though she was the youngest girl on the street. She was caught in a cruel world. There was no pity for anyone. She had thought that life at her mother's house was the lowest hell, but she had been wrong.

Tatiana was not her real name. She had changed it when she became a prostitute. Her dream was to find a good guy and to have family with him eventually, but until then she needed to survive. She started to look for Johns alone and had quickly attracted a lot of clients. She was young, beautiful and cheap. But one day, a tough guy came to her and said: "You cannot work alone, you have to work for me. I will make sure that you are always paid, and you always have clients, but you will pay me half of your income. If you are not happy with my offer, I will cut your face with this big knife." That was the moment that true hell started for her and continued for two years. She was regularly beaten and abused by her pimp and forced to become addicted to drugs. She had been enslaved.

Tatiana was also beaten by other hookers because she was younger and more beautiful than they were. One morning, she had had enough. She decided to end her misery forever. She knew that her pimp was on his way over to take advantage of her before he started his day and would find her before she was done, so she quickly left the apartment. She took a taxi to the tallest bridge in the city. As she climbed the railing and got ready to jump, she said sorry to her mother in her mind. Even though she had been a bad parent, Tatiana still loved her because she was the only mother she had. She watched the cars passing by her, but nobody paid attention. She realized that she did not belong in this cold, cruel world and she was just getting ready to jump when a guy drove up and asked her if she needed any help with committing suicide. For the first time in two years, she smiled. He had stopped his car right in the middle of the bridge, not caring about the traffic that was piling up because of him. He climbed onto the barrier and said that if she was going to jump, he was going to jump also. She looked into his eyes and she realized that he wasn't joking. She said to him "Please leave me alone, I want to die."

That was how she had first met Oleg. He looked at her and said, "Three times a day I want to commit suicide and then I think about the kids from the orphanage that I support and how are they going to manage without me? The government has almost no budget for them. How would you like to work with those kids? I would pay you a salary. By the way, my name is Oleg," he said as he stuck out his hand. She saw the tattoo on his hands and scars on his face, she figured out right away that he was a criminal and not for one second did she believe what he said, until she looked in his eyes. From all her experience as a hooker, she had developed a sixth sense on an almost magical level. All she had to do was look into the eyes of a person, and she would know exactly if the person was telling the truth or lies. Her gut was telling her that Oleg did not lie. From that point on they were inseparable.

She fell in love with Oleg because he was her rescuer and he was good to her. He paid for her rehab and helped her to find a good job. He then paid for her college education so she could become an accountant. But one day he told her that it was time for her to find a normal guy because he was going to bring her only pain and suffering. She knew that there was no future with Oleg, but she loved him with all her heart. She knew that he had cheated on her and it was simply how it was for him because of his lifestyle. He always told her that he could be locked up in jail at any time, for many years or be killed any time, so he wanted to take everything he could from life today because tomorrow might not happen. She never stopped loving him but eventually she did meet a good guy, and soon they were married.

Now Oleg was in trouble, and it was her time to pay him back, even if it cost her life. "Let's go, I am going to drive you to the hospital, and you are going to lay down on the back seat with your AK-47." He was about to argue but before he did, he looked into her eyes and recognized that same crazy look that she had on the bridge seven years ago. She was ready to die. Tatiana drove the car through the city, and for the first time in his life he prayed, "God, if you exist, please help me. I promise I will turn my life around." The police were everywhere in the city. On every crossroad and side street they could see a police checkpoint. He told himself that if their car was stopped by the police, he was going to start shooting immediately. Surprisingly, their car was not stopped.

When they arrived at the emergency ward, he saw two police cars across the street. He asked Tatiana to drop him off and come back in a couple hours. "If I am not there, go to the forest and leave the car." She was certain that this was going to be the last she would ever see of him, and she wanted to tell him so many things, but she was out of time. He tucked his gun behind his back and left the car. She opened the driver door window and shouted out, "Thank you Oleg, for everything! I love you."

When he opened the door of the emergency room, he almost lost consciousness. He had lost a lot of blood and was weak as a kitten. He kept thinking, "I made it to the hospital alive, it's already God's gift. Now all I have left to do is take the last step to survive. After, when everything is over, I'll call my guys and they'll help me."

He had to gather his strength to make it through the corridors of the hospital. He guessed which room he should go into. It was a huge gamble, but he pushed open a large door and saw three people inside the room dressed in scrubs. "Who is the doctor here?"

"I am a surgeon, this is my assistant and my theatre nurse," answered a doctor who looked about sixty-five. What are you looking for, sir?"

Oleg took out his AK-47 and put it to the head of the surgeon and said, "You will do the operation on my wound right now. If you try to call the police, I will kill everybody here!"

The doctor stared hard at Oleg, then said, "You're the guy wanted by the police." When the doctor had driven from his home to the hospital, he had seen police everywhere. He heard on the radio about the incident and when he arrived at the hospital, the news stations were talking about it nonstop. Oleg's picture had been shown on TV, so there was no question about who he was. The doctor had not expected this wanted criminal to burst into his operating room and put a machine gun to his head. He knew from the news reports that Oleg had nothing to lose and that he was not joking. The doctor called the assistant and asked her to bring everything they needed for the operation. His assistant had worked with him for over thirty-five years and by the tone of his voice she knew that something serious had happened, so she did not ask any questions, she just did what he asked.

Oleg had taken three bullets to the chest and was bleeding a lot. He was very lucky that no bullets had hit his vital organs. The doctor told Oleg that he needed to give him an anesthetic for pain so that he could stitch the wounds up properly. Oleg said, "If you do not want to have a bullet in your head, put the stitches without any pain killers and do it quickly!"

It was the fifth time that Oleg had been shot in his life. He was used to overcoming pain, but he had never had stitches without any anaesthetic. During the operation, the pain was so intense, he prayed for the second time in his life. Finally, it was over. "Give me thirty minutes before you tell the police about my visit and I promise nobody is going to touch your family." The doctor gave him some antibiotics and Oleg left the room.

When Oleg first went inside the hospital, Tatiana had taken the car and hid it in the underground parking where it couldn't be seen. She walked back to the hospital and waited for him outside, near the door to the hospital so that she would know if he came out. She did not want to stay inside the hospital in case someone started asking questions. She had already waited for over an hour in the ice-cold, but she was so stressed that she did not feel the cold. She purchased a pack of cigarettes even though she hadn't smoked for seven years. But today she needed a smoke. She found the two hours she waited the longest hours in her entire life. Every time she saw a policeman, her heart started beating faster.

Finally, she saw Oleg come out the door of the hospital. She barely recognized him. His skin was grey. When he approached her, he muttered through his teeth, "I am dying from pain, I need vodka now!" She handed him a cap and sunglasses as they walked to the car. When they drove back home, she stopped by a convenience store and quickly purchased some food and a bottle of vodka. When they arrived back at her house, it was around seven p.m. and there was a light on inside her house. Her husband was home.

Tatiana had met her husband Sergei, five years ago while she was working at the orphanage. He was a truck driver and every week he brought food for the children. He was a tall, nice-looking guy, very calm and respectful. In fact, he was the opposite of Oleg; a simple, law-abiding citizen. Sergei had not had many girlfriends before. He was shy when they started dating and she liked that in him very much. He brought her flowers and simple, inexpensive gifts, but they were given out of love, which is something she had never had before. When she broke up with Oleg, he was happy for her. He had already told her many times before to find a good guy, because she was wasting her time with him. Oleg thought that Sergei was an excellent choice for Tatiana. That is why Oleg did not want Sergei to see him and get him involved in this bad situation. He asked Tatiana to drive him to a phone booth and leave him there.

They drove in silence. Neither of them had the energy to talk. When they arrived at the phone booth, Oleg looked at her tenderly and said, "Don't worry about me, we are even now," and he left the car. She was sure that she would never see him again and wanted to ask him so many things, but she said nothing. She just watched him walking away. Tatiana drove to the forest, not far from her home, and she left the car in the woods.

When he got out of the car, he used the payphone to call all of his partners and the people who were working with him, but nobody answered. He figured that they did not want to talk to him, but how would they know that it was him calling? There was no Caller ID then. He went to the park and hid in an area where there were no lights. He had just realized that he hadn't eaten for two days. He was so exhausted that he did not even feel the pain anymore. He ate his food and drank half the bottle of vodka and suddenly he was asleep on the snowy ground. He dreamed that his wife was driving her car across the city looking for him. Then he saw, like in the movies, himself as a child playing with his mother and other kids from the building next door. He saw himself as a teenager, and his first time in juvenile prison. Then there were no more dreams. Suddenly, he felt himself flying up and away from his body. He felt freedom; no more pain, no more stress. For the first time in his life, he felt incredibly happy. He was flying so fast, all around the park, and he was laughing like a crazy man. Then, he was flying beyond the park and he saw many cars driving on the snowy roads.

"It seems like nobody can see me," thought Oleg. He saw policemen walking on the street. He shouted loudly to them, "Fuck you, you corrupted assholes! I fuck your mother, so go fuck yourself!" He made fun of them, but they did not react at all. He found that boring after a bit and wanted to see what his friends were up to, so he flew to find his best friend, Andrei. He had met him in juvenile prison and since then they stayed close. They went through hell together and always supported each other, even through their difficult moments.

When he arrived at Andrei's condo, he saw his wife in the staircase crying, with their baby wrapped in a blanket. He quickly approached her and asked her what happened and where Andrei was. She did not see him or hear his voice. Two policemen were searching the living room. They threw clothes, books - basically everything - on the floor. They broke furniture and cut the sofa and armchair up with a knife to see what was inside. Then Oleg heard the sounds of pain and fists pounding against flesh over and over and over. He turned and saw three policemen violently beating Andrei.

They wanted Andrei to tell them where Oleg was and promised to stop beating him if he did. Andrei told them that he had no idea. Oleg screamed with all his strength, but nobody heard him. He saw the chair tipped over on the floor and he tried to pick it up, but he could not. He was sad and depressed about how unfair it was. Andrei needed him now, but he couldn't do anything to help him. Oleg knew it was his fault that his friend Andrei was being harassed by the police. The police wanted him, not Andrei.

For the first time in his life, he was in a situation where he could do nothing to help. He realized that he needed to go back and find his body, wherever that was. He wasn't sure whether he was dead, having a really strange dream, or some sort of otherworldly experience. He flew through the city and on one road he saw a car driving very slowly, not far from where his body was. In the dark he could not see inside the car, so he flew back to the park, closer to his body instead. However, he suddenly had an intense desire to go back and look inside the car. It seemed familiar. He flew back and he saw that it was his wife's vehicle. It was a gift he had given her on her birthday last year. He wanted to sit next to her in the car, and right away he was inside the passenger seat. Her face was worried, and she repeated again and again, "Oleg where are you? Where are you, my love?"

He was surprised that such a fragile girl would go out in freezing cold weather, in the dark of night to look for him. She was always so scared to go out in the evening. Moreover, he had brought her so much trouble in her calm life, he knew he didn't deserve her. The last time he was in jail, she had to take two trains and walk four kilometers to bring him food. Every Saturday she came to visit him. She showed up even in snowstorms. It finally struck him that he loved her with all his heart. He knew what he needed to do. He needed to stop his criminal business. He decided he was going to find a job in construction, and they were going to make plans to start a family. He wanted to have a boy first, at least one kid for sure. They could move to another city and start over again. He was quite sure that she would be the best mother in the world.

Suddenly, he began to worry, he did not know why. There was no reason to be worried. This beautiful young girl loved him, and he loved her. The first thing he was going to do when he headed back to his body was to move them to another city. He was going to live under a different name. Then he started to wonder what exactly had happened to him. Why was he out of his body? What happened to his body while he was flying around the city? Maybe he was dead, and he is now a ghost. That didn't seem impossible, so it must only be a beautiful dream. Ghosts don't exist, Oleg said to himself. However, he began to worry more and more. Before leaving the car, he talked to his wife. "Darling, please go to Park Illiatcha and pick me up from there. We went there so many times on walks," but she did not seem to hear anything. Finally, he left the car and flew back to his body.

Oleg was so happy when he saw himself sleeping on the ground. He tried to get back into his body, but he couldn't seem to figure out how to go about it. He had a feeling that the body was not his anymore. He tried to close his eyes and open them again and again, but he got nowhere with it. This bad dream did not want to end! He tried to pound on his body or turn his head, but he couldn't seem to control anything. He sat down on his body and realized that his worst fears came true, his body was dead, and he really was a ghost. There was no way to go back.

He was so disappointed to have to die like that. He started to cry out loud like a baby, without worrying about who would hear him. He was alone and dead. He would not even care if somebody saw him crying. He had wanted to change his life, but now that was all over. He wanted to change his name and move to another city with his wife and make children and be happy. He had always told her, "Not now, soon for sure. We have lots of time, we are young." But now it was too late. He started thinking about all the people that he'd killed or injured. Most of them were not good people, but they had families, parents and loved ones. He could avoid being so cruel to them even if they did not obey him. He did that to make an example of what happens to people who do not obey him. Basically, he did it to scare others into following his orders.

He started to ask forgiveness from them. He kept thinking over and over in his mind about the moments when he was violent with people and how he would avoid those situations.

He regretted being that way very deeply in his heart. First time in his life, he was completely honest with himself. Then he lifted his head to the sky and had a talk with God. "God if you exist, give me a chance to go back to earth and change my life. I will start by helping others who are in a similar situation to change their lives and stop being criminals."

In the same moment he felt an unknown force pulling him up into the air. He did not know what exactly was going to happen but climbed into the clouds without doing anything at all. He felt like he was traveling in a hot air balloon, away from his body. His dream was to come back to earth as a human, melted like snow in the spring. "Now I will need to answer for why I did so much shit on earth," he said to himself. He saw the entrance to a tunnel coming up fast. "Be a man!" yelled Oleg to himself as he flew inside the tunnel. An unseen power pushed him through the tunnel, and he started to hear the men, women, and children's voices. They did not speak any languages at all, it was just a bunch of screams and cries. Although the tunnel was dark and he couldn't see anybody, he felt as if there were a lot of other people flying close to him.

Finally, in the distance he saw a light. He thought it was probably an exit of some kind and when he was finally out of the tunnel, he saw a magnificent paradise. There were beautiful waterfalls, mountains, and meadows with gorgeous flowers. New-born lambs grazed in the highlands, colourful birds, deer played with the children. Even in the movies, he has never seen such a beautiful and peaceful place. He landed on the grassy hillside and approached a cliff to get a better view of this paradise. Somebody touched his shoulder and he turned around to find that it was his mother. He was shocked at first, then he realized where he was, and he hugged her. "Mama, how is your life here?" asked Oleg. "I am doing well and am happy living here with your father."

Back on the hill, his mother took his hand in hers and he walked with her like when he was a small child. They went through a beautiful garden. He has never seen such colourful flowers like they had here. Further down he saw apple trees and peach trees with large, ripe fruit on them. Then he saw a magnificent house with a peaceful river passing next to it. Around fifty meters further from the house he saw a pristine wooden building. "We live here, and, in this church, we pray for you every day." When they approached the house, a nice looking, tall man opened the door and welcomed the important guest. He had only seen his father in pictures and did not recognize him right away.

He said, "Hi son, nice to meet you." and he gave him a warm hug. The house was built in an older style. The living room was large and open, with very high ceilings. They sat down on the table in front of the fireplace to get better acquainted. The house was tastefully built. "It is my dream house," thought Oleg. It seemed that his father was reading his thoughts because he smiled and said, "A house like this was my dream also. I wanted to build it for us, but I didn't have the money." Oleg asked his parents where he was going to live. His mother answered, "Your time is not up yet Oleg. We prayed extremely hard, and we fasted. Finally, God gave you a chance to go back to earth to atone for your sins. You must change your life and help others to change theirs if you are to be forgiven."

"But I do not want to go back to earth. I would like to stay here with you." Oleg pleaded. Both parents shook their heads sadly. "If you die now, you would not get to come here. You must earn the right to be here. Would you like to see where you would go if you died right now?" asked his father. "Yes," answered Oleg. "Good, follow me," said his father.

Before leaving the house, his mother approached Oleg and said, "Please remember, this is your last chance. Make good choices, we believe in you." They walked for a long time and finally they stopped at the edge of a precipice. His father watched Oleg's eyes and said, "I feel bad that I left you so early on in your life. I am sure your life would have been much different, and you wouldn't have made so many mistakes if I would have been there to guide you as you grew up. Now it's up to you to choose the right path. I did all I could to give you this chance. In a moment, someone is going to pick you up. He's going to show you something and then you will be brought back to your body." He gave his son a hug and went back to his wife.

Oleg watched his father walking away until he heard steps behind him. He turned around and saw a huge monster. It was three times as tall as Oleg, and had a human body, with big muscles and a muttons head. "Hi tourist! It's been a very long time since I've greeted a tourist. Follow me," said the monster.

"Oleg took one step forward and instantly relocated to another world. The surface of this place looked like NASA pictures of the moon. Everything was dark. Around every twenty meters you could see holes that like lunar craters, or the biggest pits on earth. Along the edges of the pits sat creatures like devils. They laughed and looked at their new visitor. Oleg approached one of the holes and he heard a high-pitched scream from the bottom. Oleg's guide told him that this is the house of adulterers. When he was closer, he found this hole significantly larger, nearly two-hundred feet. When he looked down, he screamed from the horror of what he saw there. He saw the humanoid animals were whipping and abusing the women and men. He heard the voices pleading, "Please kill me!" Oleg could not look anymore, and he turned his head away. The guide said to Oleg that they must stay there until they can go back to earth. "How long must they stay?" asked Oleg. "Nobody knows. We do not decide it," said the guide. "Who decides?" asked Oleg. "Do not ask me stupid questions," answered the guide.

They went to another hole where Oleg saw thousands of people sitting on the floor. Tubes were stuck in their throat and devils were pouring liquid inside the tubes. Oleg asked, "What is the liquid they put in?" The guide answered, "Bad quality alcohol that burns their viscera. However, they won't die, they just suffer. On earth those people were alcoholics." The people moaned, cried, and asked them to stop but the devils just laughed. The people threw up blood everywhere, on the floor and themselves. The tubes were stuck deep in their throats and there was no way to remove them.

It was a terrible sight and Oleg quickly stepped back. He asked the monster if these souls felt pain. After all, they were not human anymore. Were they? "They feel like the people they were when they were on earth. Would you like to try? If yes, just pick one of the holes," the monster said. However, Oleg did not want to try. He just asked where the place for people who killed or injured other people was. The guide said, "I can show you that quickly, but you have to go back soon."

They passed by a few holes and stopped by one larger than others. When he approached, he saw a terrible picture: it was a sea of blood. Some souls were bound to a radiator with handcuffs and demons stabbed big knives into their body. The souls lost consciousness and a few minutes later, they woke up as the demons stabbed the knives inside their body again and again. This procedure went on and on. It was horrible to watch, so he turned away. He had seen enough. He was ready to go back.

CHAPTER SEVEN

THE FIGHT TO SURVIVE

Oleg woke up and looked around him. He recognized the park where he had fallen asleep. He looked at his watch and he realized that he had only slept for about an hour. He was so cold. He got up and went towards the exit of the park. He thought about the crazy dream he just had and wondered if it was real or not as he wandered aimlessly along the road.

He couldn't get the vision out of his head. He started thinking about his father. In the dream he looked the same as in the picture that his mother had on the desk in the apartment where he grew up. Suddenly, far away he saw a car driving slowly towards him. He hid behind the bushes but even in darkness he recognized his wife's vehicle. He jumped out of the bushes and ran in front of the car. She barely had time to hit the brakes. He quickly got in the car. She hugged him and said, "I almost lost the hope of finding you!" He asked her how she knew that he was in trouble. She said that it was all over the news and his picture was in the newspapers and the grocery stores. Police were offering ten thousand dollars to the person who would tell them where he was. She figured that he needed her help and she was going to be there for him, come Hell or high water.

If he was going to fix this problem, he was going to have to start a new life. Oleg promised his wife that he was going to find a job and help others who are criminals to change their lives. She was surprised to hear this but did not say a word because she was so focused on getting him home quickly, and without running into the police. When they arrived, he undressed, climbed into bed and fell asleep right away. Olga did not even have the time to say a word to him, so she let him sleep.

She watched him for a long time and was wondering what to do. She knew that he could not stay there, because sooner or later police were going to find out where he was. If he left, police would find him and kill him right away. They would not even bother putting him in jail. She figured the best thing to do was to call the authorities in the morning and tell them that he would give himself up. She noticed that he was behaving differently, calmer somehow. He hadn't used any swear words, which was very unusual. She told herself that she would talk to him in the morning.

Oleg woke up early in the morning with a sharp pain in his side. He took the antibiotics and painkillers and was drinking his coffee when Olga walked into the kitchen. She asked him what he planned to do next. He said that he didn't have any idea, but maybe she should call the police and let them know that he was here. He had thrown the AK-47 away in the forest the previous night and he knew that when police came, he wouldn't have any guns on him. She said that she couldn't sleep last night, worrying about what to do. "Good. Tell me, what do you think I should do?" asked Oleg. She outlined exactly what she was thinking. He was surprised to see his wife so strong-willed. He did not notice those qualities in his wife before. He thought she had no opinion because she always agreed with him and never argued, but now in a critical moment, she was telling him what to do.

"Okay, first you'll need to wear your white suit. I will call a lawyer friend that I know and explain the situation to him. I will take the picture of you wearing your white suit and I am going to mail the pictures to him. When the police arrive, I will tell them what I have done and hopefully, it will stop them from killing you," said Olga. It was a bold plan because the police could easily kill him and his wife without any questions asked. "How about if I go to the police alone? I am almost certain that they are going to kill me. However, you are not involved, and you don't need to risk your life for me." He told her the situation that happened to him in the forest. Olga believed in God, and she went regularly to church so she viewed what happened as a spiritual revelation from God. She had prayed for years that Oleg would change his life and start to believe in God. She had heard many stories like that before, and she had always believed in God. She was thrilled that this had finally happened to him. "Now you believe in God?" asked Olga. "Yes, I do believe in God. That is why I am not worried about the future anymore. I am a different person now. What I want is to fix this problem and do my time and after that, start helping others," said Oleg. "Please, Oleg, listen to me and do what I tell you. My gut feeling is telling me that giving yourself up to the police is the right thing to do."

Olga took pictures of Oleg in underwear for the lawyer, then helped him get dressed in the white suit that he had worn when they had married. Oleg was still in a lot of pain. He sat in the armchair and waited while Olga went to see her lawyer friend.

Aleksei had been in love with Olga since high school. They had dated from the age of fourteen. All the girls in her class were jealous of their relationship. He was handsome, intelligent and his parents were wealthy. A bodyguard in a beautiful Mercedes picked him up from school every day.

His parents had become very successful businesspeople. They all called him a very promising fiancé. They used all their teenage wiles to tempt him into becoming their boyfriend. However, it was like Olga had cast a spell over him. He did not see anybody but her. He brought her flowers, chocolates, and teddy bears. She really thought she loved him too. After the high school prom, he invited her to his house, and they consummated that love.

After high school, she went to university to study art, and he went to law school. He wanted to marry her in the first year of university. However, his parents were against their relationship. He told them that if they were going to interfere with their relationship, he was going to leave the house. Aleksei was their only child, and they did not want to lose him. They were forced to accept his choice. He had asked her twice to marry him, but she was still not ready.

She always told him to wait until they finished university. In the last year of university was when she met Oleg - sleeping in a chair in her apartment with an open book on his lap - and she fell in love with him immediately. All of her friends and even her father told her how stupid she was to start dating a criminal. When she told Aleksei, he was terribly angry and upset with her. He took this news very badly and fell into a depression. He did not talk to her for almost six months, then he finally forgave her and within a year they were talking again. Now, she really needed his help as a lawyer. She knew in her heart that even after all these years, he was still in love with her and was hoping that it was not going to work out with Oleg. He never gave up the hope that she might someday come back to him. She dialed his office number three times, but nobody picked up the phone. She only wanted to talk to him and somehow get the camera with the pictures to him because she did not have time to develop film.

She did not have any time to lose so she took a taxi and went directly to his office. When she arrived, Aleksei was in an important meeting with one of his biggest clients and his secretary told her that she must come back tomorrow. Aleksei was not able to meet with anybody today. Olga said, "Okay," and was going towards the door to leave, when she turned around sharply and ran into the room where Aleksei was having his meeting. The secretary ran after Olga, but she was too slow for her and couldn't catch her in time.

Olga broke into the meeting room and loudly asked Aleksei to forgive her for interrupting his important meeting, but she needed to talk to him for a few minutes. He saw her eyes and he understood that something serious had happened. He asked her if she could just wait for thirty minutes. She told him that it could be too late, that is why it was an emergency. He knew this had something to do with Oleg because he had watched the latest news.

He apologized to his clients and left the room. He took her arm and they went to the next room. When he closed the door behind him, he screamed on her through the teeth, "You fucking bitch! Why are you coming here and interrupting my important meeting with your bullshit? I waited for this meeting for a whole year!"

"I'm so sorry Aleksei, for interrupting your meeting today and for everything I did to you. I know I was wrong, and I know I shouldn't have to come, but you are the only person who can help me right now. I have nobody else. You have known me for years and I have never asked you for anything. I am sure you know why I came here. It's Oleg. His life, and that means my life, is in your hands right now. If you tell me to go away, in one hour he will be dead and me too," said Olga as she started crying.

"I am so sick of your drama, Olga! Okay, I will help you because of the love that I have felt for you for so many years. However, you have to promise me that this is the last time you will ask me to help your criminal, imbecile of a husband. And then I want you out of my life forever. You only bring me problems!" yelled Aleksei, as he slapped her across the face. Olga fell to the floor and cried. He was very angry with her because she had rejected him for a low life criminal. Here he was, a successful lawyer, rich, good looking, family-oriented, and he loved her with all his heart. How could she choose a loser who was about to be killed, or at the very least, jailed for a very long time? So many beautiful and successful women wanted to be with him, and he rejected every one of them for this stupid bitch. It was so unlike him!

She reached into her bag, took a camera from it and told him, "I took the pictures of Oleg's body. I am going to call the police and when they arrive, I am going to tell them that I took the pictures of his body and gave them to you. And If they kill him now, I will tell them that you are preparing the file right now, and that they are going to be in big trouble. Promise, you are going to do it?" asked Olga, looking up at him from the ground and holding out the camera. After a long pause, he took the camera from her hand and said firmly, "I promise." She looked him right in the eyes, as if searching to see if he was telling the truth, and then left the room. Now that he was alone, Aleksei took a bottle of vodka and poured a tall glass of it and drank it all in one gulp. He didn't understand the power she had over him.

Olga took a taxi back home. When she got there, Oleg was sitting in the same position as when she had left, all curled up in the armchair. He asked her if everything was fine and she quickly answered that everything was perfect. Aleksei was going to do the job if need be. She looked him in his eyes and asked, "Are you sure that calling the police is the best solution?"

"I am one hundred percent sure," replied Oleg.

When she left the apartment, Oleg looked up into the sky and said, "God, Mother, Father, I know you are close to me now and you are watching me. If I need to die now, I am ready to do it like a man!" Olga came back in a few minutes but could not make eye contact with Oleg. She started to heat water to make coffee. Oleg felt a strange calm come over him. He had accepted the fact that this might be his time to die. Suddenly they heard a loud knock on the door. Olga rushed to Oleg and hugged him tightly. "Whatever happens, I love you and I am here for you."

She opened the door to see a dozen policemen on the staircase. They were in full protective gear and all had AK-47s in their hands. They pushed her aside, but she ran around them like a tiger protecting her cub and stood between Oleg and the policemen. She screamed, "I took many pictures of Oleg's body and my lawyer Aleksei Drozdov has copies of everything in his office. I warn you, if you kill him my lawyer is going to involve the media and send the photos to the Attorney General's office." The officers wanted to kill him so badly that they had a hard time standing still, but they did not expect that his wife would protect him like that. Even Oleg looked surprised at how brave his wife was. They could have killed them both, however, she didn't seem to fear anything or anyone at that moment.

The chief policeman ordered them to stand down. They cuffed Oleg and took him out of the apartment. Olga shouted at him as he was dragged away, "Oleg, everything is going to be fine! I will wait for you!" When they left the building, Oleg counted eleven police cars parked near his apartment building. He even saw a police helicopter hovering above. The officers put him in a patrol car and drove to the police station. While driving, they swore at him and told him that he was going to regret that he was still alive and that once they were done with him, he was going to ask them to kill him, but they would refuse. They were going to let him die a slow and painful death!

When they arrived at the police station, the officers were disappointed to discover that Oleg's lawyer had sent the pictures to the District Attorney and asked him to protect Oleg. In the former Soviet Union countries, it is particularly important to have good contacts and Aleksei had the best contacts there were in the police world. Still, they put Oleg in a strong blanket and hung him from the ceiling. They used him as a punching bag for a few minutes, then put him down and checked to see if he was still alive. After the third round, he lost consciousness. They splashed water on his face and in a few minutes, he woke up. They put him back in the blanket and brought him to the basement to an unheated concrete cell.

They used this room for "special guests." They called this room "the death room." 90% of the visitors that left the room were carried out "feet forward" while the other 10% had physical and psychological problems for the rest of their lives.

It was a small, concrete room with high ceilings and one small window with iron bars on it, near the ceiling. There was no electricity or heat, no furniture, only a hole in the floor that was used as a toilet. It was so cold inside that it eased the stench of the room.

They threw him into the death room and closed the door. After all the stress and struggling, he felt himself losing his will to live. His mind was so blank that he didn't even feel the cold and pain. He just wrapped himself in the blanket and slept.

When Oleg opened his eyes, it was morning, and the daylight was coming in through the small window. A few large rats crept from the hole in the floor and moved towards him ominously. He did not know what time it was, all he knew was that he was very cold and hungry. Because of the beating, he was in a lot of pain. His ribs were broken and his wounds were bleeding. When he breathed, he could see his breath. His body was so numbed by the cold that he just lay there not caring what happened to him and falling in and out of consciousness. Every time he woke up, he saw more and more rats coming up through the pipes and inching closer and closer to him.

He thought ruefully, it's better to freeze to death rather than be eaten alive by rats. He checked the floor for some kind of weapon and found that in some places there were deep cracks in the floor. He smashed the floor with his foot and took a few pieces of concrete with sharp edges on them. He broke a bunch of pieces off, collecting a pile of concrete chunks. As the rats got bolder, he threw the carefully aimed pieces of concrete at them. He tried to hit the biggest one first and soon the rats were scurrying for the safety of the hole in the floor. When the rats were gone, he was exhausted from all the activity and it was dark outside. The only good thing was that he was not cold anymore. He was sweaty, thirsty and hungry.

Finally, he heard someone opening the slider in the door. The guard looked surprised that Oleg was even alive. He shoved a dirty tray through the slot that held a bowl of soup, one piece of stale bread and a glass of water. The soup was a simple broth with potatoes and water. It was barely edible, but Oleg gobbled it down in under a minute.

A few hours later, he heard voices outside the door of the cell. Someone tried to open the cell door with a few keys before they gave up trying. From their voices, he realized that they wanted to kill him but not shoot him. It sounded like they wanted to hang him. Oleg said to himself, "When the first guy steps into the cell, I'm going to throw a cement piece at the head of the lucky guy, then I'm going to slit my wrists before they can do me any more damage. I won't let them take me alive!"

It was taking quite a while for the guards to open the door. They seemed to be having trouble finding the right key. He found that bizarre and started to thank God that they were struggling. Finally, they stopped trying to open the door and left him alone. That night was very difficult. He couldn't sleep because it was ice cold inside the cell. In the morning it warmed up when the sun came in the window and he fell asleep from pure exhaustion.

While in that death room, Oleg had a dream that helped

save his life. In his dream, he saw his mother sitting with him at the table in the apartment where he was born. She said to him, "My lovely son, I know what you are going through. I know you are ready to give up. You finally feel warm and happy. However, it is an illusion! If you do not wake up right now you are going to die. Please, my son. If you die now, you won't learn the Great Truth and you will not be able to teach people about that. It is called The Power of Mind. Everything can be changed in your life if you believe. Imagine that you are sitting in your cell, the door is open, and you see a nurse who is going to take care of your wounds and release you from this place of death. If you truly believe, it will happen right now. Feel it as if it happened already. Think that you are released from jail and you will come back to your wife so you can start helping other people who are in the same situation that you've been in."

Oleg started to feel the cold and he woke up slowly. He did not know what to think about his dream. He found it bizarre. He felt like his mother was laughing at him gently. He asked himself if it was truly his mother in the dream or was it a devil in the guise of his mother? He did not feel well. He had difficulty breathing because of the broken ribs. His wounds would not stop bleeding and he was both hungry and thirsty. He did not care any more about the rats. There were so many rats, they were crawling over top of each other in the room. He tried to will himself to die, but he could not.

Oleg couldn't get what his mother had said out of his head. The dream seemed so real. He said to himself, "Hell, why not follow her advice, at least I will die happy." He visualized himself leaving this death room and driving to his home. He saw his wife opening the door. He imagined them eating dinner together and talking about their future. He saw himself opening a center to help ex-prisoners. He had never been as happy as he was at this moment. He held the feeling of happiness in his heart for a few minutes, then a rat ran across his aching body and reality hit him hard. He started again from the beginning, imagining being happy with his wife and working in this center for ex-prisoners. He got the happy feeling again and his heart warmed. With the help of willpower, he was able to keep the happy feeling for a longer time. In his vision he received and gave love to many people.

He had opened himself up to a new world. Just from positive thinking, he was being born again. He hadn't ever realized that he could feel so happy just from positive visualizations. Here he was in inhumane condition, a place filled with death, and it didn't bother him anymore. He stopped throwing cement bits at rats and started to talk to them. He was talking to them about his future. They were his first listeners. Physically, he began to feel much better and started walking around his room. To ward off the cold he began to exercise.

A few hours later, the door of the cell opened, and the overseer said to Oleg that a nurse, Svetlana, was coming to check on his health. He thought that must be a dream, but it was real. Svetlana was around fifty-five years old and she bandaged his wounds and asked him when the last time he ate was. One hour later, they brought him much better food and bigger portions! Before he fell asleep, he said out loud, "Thanks, mama! For teaching me something new!"

He woke up to the sound of the door opening and saw Aleksei, his lawyer, standing in the doorway. Aleksei started talking to him. Oleg did not follow him in the beginning because he was very sore, tired, and disoriented but Aleksei kept asking questions and slowly, Oleg became more attentive. Basically, the lawyer asked what happened when he arrived, how he was being treated, how long he spent in this cell, and so on. After speaking to him for over a half an hour, Oleg was exhausted. The only thing he really wanted from Aleksei was to be moved out of this ice-cold cell. He was chilled to the bone and wasn't sure how much longer he could take it.

Aleksei promised Oleg that he was going to fix everything by the end of the day. Aleksei was a smart guy and wanted popularity. Also, he knew that Oleg was respected in the criminal world and it was always beneficial to be on good terms with those types of people. He knew that the people from his world do not forget favors. Who knows what can happen in the future? It wouldn't hurt to have Oleg in his debt. In addition to that, the District Attorney was in competition with the policeman that Oleg had killed - involving one of the turf wars - so he was happy that the officer was dead. Police chased criminals - killing them or putting them in jail - to take over their businesses. He was in a win-win situation.

Aleksei called his other friend from the department and explained to him everything that had happened to Oleg. His buddy, an attorney general, liked the idea of involving the media but hesitated to make a final decision. Oleg's file was already in the public eye, so he had to be careful how it was handled. Of course, nobody cared what happened to Oleg, it was really just about the war between a couple of police departments. Oleg was merely a pawn. At the same time, the attorney general did not want to draw too much attention to the case because maybe the mayor of the city might get involved and launch his own investigation. He did not want that.

He called his friend and colleague and explained the situation. His friend told him that this case is already public enough and everybody knows what happened. He does not need to 'put more butter on the bread', so to speak. At the same time, it was no good for anybody if Oleg died. He reasoned that if he saved Oleg's life, it might be possible to spin the story to show how humane he was before the election and at the same time show his enemies that he still had power and needed to be respected.

When Aleksei left Oleg's cell, Oleg did the same exercise as he did the day before. However, today he was able to keep the same happy feeling even longer. He was dreaming about having a happy life with his wife and having a son together with her. He saw his son growing up, finishing school, going to university, then getting married and having two children. It was especially cold in his cell, but he did not feel it like he did before. He felt happy, and now he was actually laughing!

That evening, Oleg was moved to a cell upstairs. Compared to the basement cell, it seemed like a luxurious apartment. There was a table, a chair, and a soft bed and most importantly it was warm! He was sent to shower with nice clean water and afterwards, the nurse rebandaged his wounds.

It was announced that the next afternoon he would be moved to the regular jail, and he would be held there while he waited to go to court. After a good chicken dinner, he slept like a baby. Around five a.m. he woke up. He still could not believe that he had survived the inhuman living condition of the basement cell and wasn't sleeping on the concrete floor anymore. He was a smart guy and understood that political games were being played behind his back. He knew very well that in this world, a human life is virtually worthless. Also, he knew that the good times were gone forever and that now the retribution of the criminal world would begin. He tried to think positive and focused only on positive thinking, but the reality was scary. He knew that nobody cared about his life, so his future was unpredictable.

The one thing he was scared of in jail was "press chata." It is a prisoner cell where the laws of the criminal world are not respected. The boss of the "press chata" was related to the administration of jail. If Oleg was sent there, they could do anything they wanted to him, and the administration of the prison would sanction it. He would easily be killed.

Around nine the next morning, Oleg was transported to the city prison. The prisoners already knew that Oleg was coming and in which cell he was going to be placed. He was lucky that he was placed in a normal cell, not a "press chata."

Oleg was not at the top of the criminal hierarchy in this place. However, he was still respected in the criminal world. That meant that he would not have to work in jail. By the criminal rules, he was actually not even allowed to work. The prison administration knew about these rules and allowed them. They also allowed "care packages" from outside for those special inmates. For example, they were allowed to have very good food, alcohol, drugs and even women. In return, the criminals maintained order in jail.

After killing the police superintendent, Oleg won even more respect in the criminal world and the right prisoners welcomed him with open arms. Oleg had access to restaurant food, cigarettes, alcohol, drugs, and prostitutes. Oleg had many years ahead of him to spend behind bars, but he was still finding ways to make himself comfortable.

CHAPTER EIGHT

THE FIGHT FOR CHANGE

Thankfully, I did not spend any time in prison. My closest experience to an institution like that was when I worked in psychiatry as an attendant. I was with patients all the time and I knew that most of them would never leave that place, like they were prisoners. There were times when I had contracts with only one patient. During those contracts I had to do their assessments, in order to make sure that this person wouldn't harm other patients or themself. I worked in the psych ward for six years. When I had contracts with only one patient, my job was to take care of them until they felt better and didn't need to be watched around the clock. I had to observe the patient all day, every day, everywhere they went: the washroom, bathroom, the personal room, kitchen, etc. The reason is because those people might be violent to other people or themselves or could even commit suicide.

I remember one summer; I had a contract with one lady who went by the name of Janet. This lady was around sixty years old. Every year, she spent three or four months in the psych ward. It is because when she was out of the hospital, after a certain time she stopped taking her medication. As a result, she became violent in public places and had to go back to the hospital again. That was her routine for thirty years.

Janet was not an easy-going person. It was difficult for the nurses and psychiatrist to find the right attendant for her.

She hated them all and was aggressive towards them. None of the workers wanted to take care of her. Basically, every week she ended up getting a new attendant because they would all quit but surprisingly, with me she was nice and I spent a month with her. We had a good time together and she talked openly about her life. We became almost like friends. I remember one evening, she wanted to take a bath and I told her, "No problem, Janet," and due to the procedure, I had to be almost inside the bathroom. "That's okay," she said. She knew the protocol, went to the bathroom, and put water into the bathtub.

I saw a lot of steam coming up from the bath and I worried that the water was too hot. I asked her, "Janet, are you sure the water isn't too hot? Do I need to check?" but she said, "No, no. You don't need to check it. Everything is fine," and I saw her climb into the bath quickly.

She spent over half an hour in this water and even fell asleep. I had to call her name to wake her. When she left the bath, I had to make sure that everything was cleaned up. The water was not released from the bath because she did not take the bathtub stopper out. I put on gloves and tried to open the stopper in the bathtub, but quickly had to pull my arm back because the water was extremely hot. I could not even put my hands into the water without burning my skin.

I came to Janet and asked her, "What happened with the water? It's too hot! I could not even open the stopper to let the water out," and Janet said, "Oh, I can do it. The water is not hot at all. It's even a little bit cold now." She opened the stopper and I checked again. The water was still scalding hot! I asked Janet, "What happened Janet? How could you stay in there for so long? You must have burned your skin." I checked her body and it was not red at all.

It made no sense to me how she could stay for thirty minutes in very hot water like that. In her mind the water wasn't hot at all - it was a bit cold - and she was worried that she was going to get sick because of it. I could not explain it.

After that, Janet left our department to move to a different ward before she was released from the hospital, so I lost contact with her. I thought about this situation for some time and discovered that there are very few people in the world - who have done yoga for many years or other types of meditation - and they can tell their mind things like, "The water is not hot," and they can stay for a long time in extremely hot water with no trouble at all. But Janet never did yoga or meditation and didn't work with her mind. She simply believed that the water was not hot and maybe even a little bit cold. I thought more about this, and I came to the conclusion that everyone has a superpower if they don't block it.

Our minds have huge power. All that we need to do is to trust our superpower potential. I talked to other nurses about the situation with Janet and all of them told me that it was true, that even a psychiatrist had told them to let her take a bath at whatever temperature she feels comfortable with because she would not take a bath in normal temperature. They said that many times the doctors inspected Janet's body after taking a bath in scalding water and they did not find anything wrong with her at all! What feels unbearable to many people may feel just right to someone else. Most of the time, we are capable of changing how we feel about the world.

After one year of working in Germany, I decided not to extend the contract with the hospital.

I was glad to finally go back home. Once I was back in Odessa, I did not know what to do with myself. I remember it was summertime. I did not have any money but now I could stay in a beautiful, newly renovated apartment with my parents. My dad was a very good renovation carpenter and they purchased new furniture, so it was like living in a luxury apartment.

I looked around for work and found out that in Odessa, there were many ethnic Germans living there with descendants who immigrated to the Russian empire centuries ago. I also found out that many of them were in prison in GULAG because of their nationality. At that time, I was almost fluent in German so I wrote a business plan that explained how I could help the old, poor, ethnic Germans in Odessa. In my city, there is a really old German church, and I presented my plan to the Episcopal of the church. To give me a better chance, I told him that my mother was half German, which was not true, but I thought it would help get me a contract.

They liked the idea, they liked me, and they started financing my project. They gave me the addresses of around a dozen old people who were living in a bad financial condition because they had been targeted by the Soviet regime. I brought food to those people every day, sometimes cleaned their apartments, cut their toenails, and did their health massages among other things. But what they enjoyed the most was when they would tell me their stories, because they did not have anybody to share them with. Their life stories were all tragic.

For example, one old man that I visited was arrested at the age of sixteen by the Police of Soviet Union (NKVD). The reason for his arrest? He could speak German and was intelligent, so he spent two decades in GULAG. His family did not know what was happening with him during this time. When he finally came back home, his family did not even recognize him. He was only thirty-six years old at that time, but he looked like a seventy-year-old man.

Every one of these people had crazy life stories but now nobody cared about them. I helped the old people in Odessa for four years. I gathered a good team of five students who helped me with this project and supported around twenty elderly citizens. Everything was good with this project, and I built good and trustful relationships with charity organizations in Germany as well as Austria, who regularly helped finance our project. The students who helped me were responsible and hard workers which made my job easier. But I was not happy and do not know how to explain why. It felt good to help people but at the same time I felt that it was not my place in life and that I should be doing something different, but I didn't know what. I decided that for now I would keep doing this job, until something happened. Three years later, I met Sarah - a Canadian girl from Quebec - at an American friend's party in Odessa. She came to Odessa to learn Russian. The relationship with her brought me something new in my life. I will admit that because of my inferiority complex I did not have a lot of sexual experience. I had had sex with other women, but it was quick and a bit boring until I met Sarah.

I had no idea how to enjoy life and had always tried to stop myself from feeling any pleasure. I did not have any relationship with girls until the age of eighteen. So, I did not realize that if you meet a girl and enjoy the nice - and of course sometimes difficult - moments together, that it was normal. In addition to that, I was still very dependent on other people's opinions. To please them, I looked for girls who are beautiful in other people's eyes. I did not care about my own opinion, what I liked, and what I wanted. Honestly, I didn't even know what I liked. I started to date, not because I wanted to, but because everybody else did it. When I went on a date with the first girl in my life, I did not know what I was supposed to do with her. Once, she asked me why I could not say "I love you." I had no answer for her. I did not understand what love was. For me, relationships were like a class or a sport that was a challenge. I did not realize that I could simply enjoy life without viewing it as a competition. I did not know myself, I didn't even try to understand my feelings, what I was looking for in a relationship, or even what kind of fun activities I would like to do to make us both happy. Of course, with that kind of thinking I could not make anybody happy.

I terrorized myself and terrorized all the people around me. Girls could not understand or help me. After a few months we would break up. They didn't know why I complicated my life so much. I tried to control everything in my life to the point where I unconsciously had a grimace on my face all the time. I did not realize that I was destroying my own life and making everyone miserable.

In relationships, I expected something all the time. For example, if I texted a girl, I did not know if I really wanted to text her. It came into my mind as "I have to," and of course, I expected that she would reply right away and if she did not,

I would be angry with her. I would then have a lot of negative emotions swirling around in my head. For example, if she was not doing what I expected, I thought she didn't love me and didn't care about me. I would start to think that she was a bad person for me, and I should stop seeing her, but it was only my bad imagination. In my head, I made a big thing out of nothing, and I could not sleep or do anything else. I became obsessed and could not stop thinking about it.

But this little Canadian girl Sarah *enjoyed* making love. It was something new in my life. Because of her, I started to realize that people have sex just to enjoy and to have fun and not because they have to do it. This was something new for me.

Sarah was a student at that time, and she had to write a thesis for her master's degree diploma. So, she decided to write about human trafficking in Odessa. Odessa is a port city, and a lot of girls go from there to Turkey or the Middle East for work. Most of them go there for work as a waitress or babysitter but many of them become the victims of criminals. These people would take the girls' passports and make them work as prostitutes.

There were a few Managing General Agents that worked for non-profit organizations and were supposed to help these victims. They received a lot of financial support from Western countries. Sarah could speak in Russian very well but she asked me to go with her to interview the managers or directors of these MGAs who were supposed to help these women. We met two directors from two different organizations. Their offices had expensive renovations and their representatives wore high-end jewelry and drove luxury cars. They were very unfriendly with us and did not want to give any information about what they were doing. You could tell how corrupt they were. Nobody really knew how they were making their money and no one would tell us anything but they were all very rich.

CHAPTER NINE

THE FIGHT FOR A NEW HOME

After this situation, Sarah was depressed about corruption and did not want to stay in the Ukraine anymore. She told me she wanted to go back to Canada. I thought about it and decided, why not? We were in love and wanted to be together, but not in the Ukraine. We got married and immigrated to Quebec City. I learned French extremely fast because everybody spoke French to me and of course, I worked hard to pick up on it. Within five months, I was almost fluent and started to work in a psychiatric hospital as an attendant. At the same time, I became a full- time student at Université Laval in the social work faculty.

It was a difficult time, with years of work and study ahead of me. The work in the hospital allowed me to pay my tuition fees and four years later I finished university without debt and had my bachelor's degree in social work.

In one of the wards where I worked, there was a lady, we can call her Christine. She was an old lady that lived in the psych ward permanently. I often worked in the evening. After the patients were asleep, we had almost nothing to do and we just talked to each other. I became friends with one of the workers, and she told me a story about Christine. Christine was a lovely lady who in the past had been incredibly talented and successful in real estate. Everything was easy for her and she had such a bright future. She was also kind of a magician.

In the hospital, there was one guy whose name was David who worked there as a janitor. David was a very funny guy. He liked to talk to the workers and patients and made everyone laugh. They loved him and always waited for him to come to work. Christine liked him a lot and one day she said to him, "David, I will make you rich."

Of course, he found it funny because he did not believe it and he made a lot of jokes about it. He would say, "Yes! It worked, Christine! Now I am extraordinarily rich. I am a millionaire and I can do everything I want! All of my salary here now goes to charity!" Everybody laughed. He made a lot of jokes like that to everyone. Sometimes, he would ask her for fun, "Christine, when will you really make me rich? Tell me." And she always said, "The time has not arrived yet."

It was months later when Christine said, "Come to my room." David came to her room and she gave him a paper with a series of numbers on it. She advised him to play the lottery and use those numbers that she gave him. He took the paper but did not use it. He just brought it home, put it in a desk drawer with other papers, and he forgot about it, but he continued to do the jokes even more. He would say, "I won the lottery and I am a *multi*-millionaire!" He repeated that a lot. So everybody started calling him Mister Millionaire.

One day, he was exercising at home with weights, and suddenly the weight fell from his hand onto the desk. The desk was broken and he didn't have any choice but to throw it away. So, first he took all his documents from the desk and he found the paper with the numbers that he had received from Christine. After thinking for a few minutes, he threw the paper in a trash can.

During dinner, he mentioned to his wife what happened to the desk and told her that he found Christine's paper. His wife said he should fish the paper out of the trash, go to the store, buy a lottery ticket, and use Christine's numbers. He didn't want to do it, but she convinced him to try. He found the crumpled paper with the numbers, went to the store, and got the ticket.

He ended up winning eight million, six hundred forty-five thousand dollars! David claimed his prize and there was an article in the newspaper about him. After winning the lottery, unfortunately, he forgot about Christine right away and quit his job. He did not even say thank you to her. Christine used to tell him, "When you become a millionaire, you have to give some money to charity. A minimum of ten percent. It's very important. It's called tithing," and of course, he said, "Yes, I will do it for sure," but when he won those millions, he did not give one dime to charity. He purchased a few rental properties and invested money in businesses instead.

That was all the information I got from my colleague at the time. Of course, she lost all connection with him. This story impressed me but like everything, I started to forget about it and I continued to live my life.

A few years later, I started to work in a community organization with homeless people. There, I met an educator named David, who was very professional. At the same time, he was funny and easy going. It was a pleasure to work with him. We became friends, and sometimes we went to the pub on Fridays, but he would never drink alcohol. Only juice. He said that he did not like alcohol.

One day after work, we went for a beer and I asked him about his life and what he did before this job as educator. He told me I probably wouldn't believe him but that he had won over eight million dollars. Eight million, six-hundred forty-five thousand dollars to be exact. I was surprised, and I told him the story about a person named David from the hospital where I worked. His expression became sad and I saw the tears on his face...

He was the same David who used to work in the hospital as a janitor.

I asked him what happened to him after winning the lottery. He told me that after getting the money, he traveled for a few months with his wife and their baby. After coming back, he purchased a few income properties, a few liquor stores, and other businesses, like restaurants, etc. Everything was good for the first year but then he found new friends because he did not want to associate with his old, poor friends, and he stopped talking to his parents. He found them to be useless and not smart because they kept giving him stupid advice like to save his money and give some money to charity.

The new friends were teaching him how to live his life to the fullest. He started to drink a lot of alcohol, did drugs and cheated on his wife. When he was sober, which was seldom, he realized that his life is going downhill fast. But in those moments, he blamed his wife because she convinced him to use Christine's numbers and win the lottery. They were much happier when they were poor, and now with millions in the account, he was miserable.

As a result of his cheating, his wife left him, but he did not care about it at the time. He started to use all kinds of drugs and he became heavily addicted. He ended up with a lot of legal problems and within a few years, he lost all of his buildings and businesses. His new friends took advantage of him and stole the last of his money and he became almost homeless. He didn't even have enough money to pay his rent. There he was, an addict and an alcoholic, with no more money. If he didn't have enough money to buy heroin, he would buy cheap vodka and get drunk. He remembered one day in winter when none of the shelters would allow him access because he was too aggressive and drunk and that night he almost died because of the cold.

He told me that was the night that changed his life. For the first time ever, he prayed to God and asked for help. He thought a lot about his life and what he did to his family and friends. In the morning, he decided to walk to his parent's house. He had to keep walking during the night on the empty streets so he wouldn't freeze.

David had not seen his parents since shortly after he had won the lottery. He was hungry and hadn't eaten for a few days. It was the end of the month and he only had enough money for alcohol and drugs, not enough for food. Finally, after a few hours walking in the ice-cold weather, he reached his parent's house and collapsed in their front yard. He was falling asleep from the cold and was extremely exhausted. He could feel death coming for him but he gathered up his last bit of strength and got on his knees. He could not cry anymore, he just stayed on his knees. At that moment, he was ready to die.

When his mother opened the door, she saw him but she did not recognize him for a few seconds. When she did, she fainted. When David's father came to the door, he pulled his son into his arms and brought him inside the warm house. When David was safe and warm, he kissed the feet and hands of his parents and asked them for forgiveness. He was ready to turn his life back around.

In the next few days, he apologized to his ex-wife, his son, and his friends. Everyone was happy that he was back! He went to rehab and has not done drugs or alcohol for seven years. He became a good father to his son, who is a teenager now, and spends most of his time with his family. After rehab, he went to college and became an educator. Since then, he started working with homeless people. Also, after rehab, he finally went back to the hospital to visit Christine to say thank you. He told her his story and Christine listened attentively.

When he finished, she said to him, "Do you remember I told you to give to charity and do volunteer work? The Universe gave to you and you have to give back."

He asked her how she knew the numbers for the lottery ticket. She said that she did not know if they were winning numbers, she just basically made those numbers up. But she knew his personality and she knew that he would keep saying he was a millionaire for fun. She said, "The universe listens to our words and listens to our wishes. Our mind has a lot of power, so everyone has to be careful what they ask for."

After meeting Christine, he understood that he could help people in need who did not believe that they had the power to change their own lives. That is the reason why he decided to become an educator.

I think Christine was a good psychologist - rather than some type of magician - and she knew about the power of the mind. She knew David's personality and she knew that he was going to joke about winning the lottery. That meant he was going to program himself for success. She told David when he visited her for the last time that the universe was listening to us and we have to be very careful what we say and what we wish for.

Unfortunately, my personal life was not as successful as professional life. My wife and I were not happy together. We both had bad tempers, and no one wanted to compromise so we did not get along very well. We were always fighting and did not have any love for each other, so we finally divorced. We are still good friends, and I maintain a close relationship with her parents to this day, but we were not good together as a couple so I moved out and focused on finishing my schooling so I could still support my family.

After finishing my study in university, I started to work as a social worker in the Ministry of Youth and Child Services in Gaspésie, which was an eight-hour drive from Quebec City. My son was only four months old at the time and I found it was very difficult for me to be so far away from him. Also, I was disappointed with the work that I was doing. I got the feeling that I was working with my computer and not with people. We had to answer hundreds of questions on the computer before making a decision. Basically, it was too much office work for me, and I wanted to work with people directly. Anyway, after three months, I came back to Quebec

City and looked for a job. However, all I found was work with the Ministry of Youth and Child Services. I did not have any choice but to accept this job because I had a baby to take care of and the mother of my son was a full-time student in university.

One year later, I realized that I should quit this job. It was a difficult decision to make especially when you have a young child. So, I had to decide on my own. I said to myself, "If I do not quit now, I will end up doing what I do not like forever!" When I studied social work in university, it was interesting: we learned psychology, relationships, and how to help people. But in real life, I was sitting for hours in my office in front of my computer, completing hundreds of questionnaires. I did not have time to see the clients. I had basically wasted four years of university and one year working as a social worker before I realized it was not for me. It was so frustrating! But I preferred to lose five years rather than waste my entire life. I knew that in forty years I would never forgive myself if I did not take a risk because I was too scared to leave my comfort zone. I asked myself, "Why did I leave the Ukraine?" The answer was, to find myself and to be happy in my skin and to feel useful. I knew that I couldn't realize my talent doing this job. I felt like I was a prisoner of stupid rules of bureaucracy! We were supposed to help people, not just police them, but I knew that alone I could not go against the system.

It was a difficult decision to make but I decided to change my profession. After a few months of research, I decided to become a financial advisor. I decided to help people who wanted to be helped. Of course, it was a completely different field of work, but I have never been scared of difficulty and I took on this challenge with all of my strength. Everyone who knew me did not understand my decision to give up stable work to start a new career where I wouldn't have any experience, but I did not see myself doing this office work forever. I would not be happy doing it either. I knew that what I really wanted to do was work one-on-one with people.

I took a six-month introductory course to become a financial advisor, passed five exams, and became a licensed financial advisor by the end of that year. A new life and new challenge! As a financial advisor I was paid entirely by commission, so I had to sell to survive. In order to make money, I had to go out and find my own clients because nobody would give them to me and they would not just come knocking on my door or call me up to buy life insurance from me. Honestly, when I changed professions, I did not even think about that. In addition to that, I had to face another hard reality: I was an immigrant in Quebec City (not all people there liked immigrants) and I did not have many friends. Especially to whom I could sell life insurance. My manager told me, "Because you are an immigrant, in order to be successful you will have to work twice as hard as a local guy, and you have a family and parents to support, so get out there on the streets and find clients!"

CHAPTER TEN

THE FIGHT FOR EMPLOYMENT

Back when I was around fourteen or fifteen years old, I tried to sell books on the street with my friend. It was November or December, and it was so cold. We walked all day long from morning until evening for two days. Most of the people told us, "Go fuck off, we do not need your fucking books." We did not sell one single book in those two days, but an interesting thing happened on the second day of our work. That evening, we were very exhausted, so we did the door-to-door in commercial offices. After giving my speech, one owner of the business told me that I was a good salesman and I had a bright future. No, he did not purchase any books from me, but I never forgot what he told me.

I did not know that fifteen years later I would be selling door-to-door again, but in a different country with a different language. I remember my first day of going door-to-door in Quebec. It was morning, -25 degrees Celsius, but because of the high level of humidity, it felt much colder. There was a lot of snow, it was cold and windy, and nobody was on the street. I drove to an area of detached houses where I could do the door-to-door. I knew my speech perfectly and had rehearsed how I would approach the people who opened the doors of their houses.

During the time I drove, I wanted to repeat the speech, but negative thoughts kept coming into my head. "What the fuck are you doing? You are a fucking idiot!" I said to myself. "You could be working as a social worker sitting in a nice, warm office. You spent so much time, money, hard work to get the bachelor's degree in social work and now you are doing the door-to-door in ice cold weather? It is a humiliation! You are such a loser! What happens if someone from university sees you while you are doing door-to-door sales? They are going to think that you are an idiot and a loser."

I almost cried. Inside my head the voice kept yelling, "Stop the car, go back home and send out your CV to get a job as a social worker." I stopped the car and closed my eyes. I thought about my life: it had always seemed so difficult and I had so many obstacles to overcome. It all seemed too hard. I felt like giving up, so I started talking to God. I asked him one simple question, "Why do I have so many difficulties in my life?" The answer came in my mind right away, "You are not scared to be honest with yourself about your unhappiness." It is true, I met so many people in the hospitals and other places where I used to work or people that I met everywhere in the world, and wondered, "Are they happy? Have they found their place in life and do they realize their potential? Do they make an effort to find their talent and use it to the maximum?" The answer was, "No!" The most that people had was a stable job. Even if they did not like it, they were doing it because it paid the bills and it was too hard to face the truth. "Nobody wants to go out of their comfort zone," I told myself, "I am different from others. I am special. I will do everything to realize my dreams, to realize my potential. I am the boss of my life. No excuses or life circumstances will prevent me from moving forward towards my dreams of being happy!"

It was an extremely difficult time for me during those months. For the first five days there were no sales. I had to do the door-to-door almost every day from early morning until I could not walk or talk anymore. I remember that after prospecting for six hours on the street, my jaw would be frozen. I could not open my mouth properly and I did not feel my toes anymore. In addition to the ice cold, I had to overcome pain in my right leg. No one knew that while I was walking, my leg hurt horribly because of the bone illness I had when I was young. I talked to everybody I could find about insurance products, everywhere I went.

I soon realized that it is not shameful to talk to people about life insurance, but it is shameful to not provide food for your family. And so, I started to sell like crazy! I found clients on the bus, at the gas station, on the street, in playgrounds where I went with my son, libraries, swimming pools, grocery stores. I became the best salesman in my insurance company among new advisors who had been in the industry for only a year.

Within two years, I had over three hundred clients, with residual income over $30,000 per year. With new sales and my residual income, I now had a good life. I supported my parents, traveled to exotic destinations, and bought an expensive car. Business was good, but my personal life was still not so good.

CHAPTER ELEVEN

THE FIGHT FOR RESPECT

I saw Oleg again after my grandfather died. My grandfather was like family to Oleg even though they were not blood relatives. When my grandfather passed away, I flew from Quebec to the Ukraine to visit my family and we went to his funeral. After the funeral, again I spent all night talking with Oleg and he told me more of his life story. Although things were difficult for me in Canada, my struggles were nothing compared to what he had gone through to gain his freedom again in Russia.

After he was sentenced, Oleg told me that he was sent to jail for eight years. He was running with his old crowd and started to drink alcohol and take drugs like he used to. He didn't care that the other prisoners worked like dogs and ate like homeless people. They were given old bread, vegetable soup and potato, while he played cards all day and dined on caviar and vodka. His wife visited him every week and soon she became pregnant. She saw that Oleg had gone back to being the same person as he was before, and eventually, she stopped visiting him. He didn't care much about that. In his debauchery of alcohol and drugs he had forgotten about the visionary experience he had about heaven, and the advice he got from his mother when he was almost dead in an ice-cold cell. He started to think that it must have just been a dream.

One day, Oleg walked in the courtyard and he saw some prisoners renovating one of the large rooms. He asked them what they were doing and they told him that it was being turned into a church. He asked them if they needed anything. They said that they need sandpaper, paint, and other construction materials. Oleg arranged for them to get everything they needed and that made him feel good. He figured that his gangster friends might find out that he had helped the guys with the construction materials, but he figured it was okay because a lot of criminals donated to churches or charity organizations.

When the church was finally opened, Oleg was invited to attend the first service. He didn't want anyone to know that he went to church and declined their offer. However, he still went every Sunday and hid near the windows. After every church service, he asked himself if he was living the right way. It became more and more difficult for him to follow his friends in everyday life. He eventually stopped using drugs and drank less alcohol. He called his wife and apologized for falling off the wagon. His son had already been born and Oleg wanted to see him.

His friends began to notice the changes in his behavior. One Sunday, they followed him to find out where he was going every week. They confronted him about his visits to the church and let him know that they didn't approve of it. It wasn't normal. He told them that it was his life and he did not care what they wanted him to do or not do.

Several months passed and Oleg started to openly go to the church. Slowly he became friends with some of the members. The criminals gave him an ultimatum. If he wanted to stay in the criminal world he would have to stop going to church and being friends with the members of the congregation or he would become like a normal prisoner and would lose any privilege he currently had in jail. His colleagues gave him five days to decide what he wanted to do. He knew exactly what that would mean. If he decided to remain a Christian, that would mean that he was leaving the criminal world forever. Even outside of prison, everybody would know about that, and it would be almost impossible to get back into the criminal world again. He might even be killed.

He'd been in the criminal world since he was very young. He hadn't studied anything in his life and didn't have any kind of profession. What was he going to do? How would he take care of his family? A few years ago, when he promised God that he was finished with crime, it was a much easier decision.

He did not sleep for three days because the pressure of his decision was weighing heavily on him. All of his criminal friends started acting very cool towards him and basically ignored him. He also got a letter from outside the prison from his business partners. They told him that they needed him because there were going to be a lot of changes over the next few years. Also, some of his friends were trying to become policemen and others were going into politics. So, when Oleg was free, they were going to do the same criminal activities they did in the past, but now it was going to be legal so he wouldn't have to risk losing his freedom.

They had been a part of his life for over twenty years, and they didn't want him to leave them at this very important moment in time. They told him that they were going to take care of his wife and kid while he was in jail so that he didn't have to worry about them. They were already in contact with the right people so he would be released from jail much earlier. They had struggled so hard to get to this point and change their life for the better, and they didn't want him to miss out. There is also a spiritual bond that holds together a criminal organization, especially in Russia, where loyalty to religion is often seen as anti-social. Basically, they tried everything to keep him on their side. For the first time in his life, Oleg had a really hard time making his decision. It really was a huge turning point. Not only did he not sleep, he also could not eat. Sometimes he had the feeling that he should stay in the criminal world and other times he convinced himself that the right thing to do was to leave that world behind and make this change in his life. However, he had another feeling that he was fooling himself and would not actually change anything. Not unless he did it right away.

He asked God why he was pushing him to make this decision in such a difficult moment, while he was in jail. He did not hear any answer. However, it felt that God started to talk to him through his heart. He asked himself where his friends had been when he was being chased by the police. The only person who was really there for him when he was in trouble was his wife. If he continued to do what he did before, what kind of legacy was he going to leave after his death? What was his son going to think about him? If what he saw in the afterlife happens to bad people after their death, what kind of torment would he go through after he died? He loved his wife and his son, and he wondered how good it would be to have a normal family. He missed his father a lot through all of his life and now he had a chance to be there for his son like his father had never been. Oleg realized that the biggest problem he had now was that he didn't believe in himself. He didn't believe that he could succeed without the criminal world. He thought about the positive qualities that he had. He was very intelligent, he learned very quickly, and he was a hard worker. If he used his potential and talents in the right direction, he could achieve a lot in his lifetime.

Oleg told me that he started to do the same exercises as he did when he was in the death cell. He visualized himself working in construction. Later he imagined himself working with a team of workers. They were building big houses and he saw himself becoming wealthy doing work that was legal and satisfying. He even saw himself opening his first rehabilitation center for ex-cons. And he imagined having two children. He visualized being happy with his wife and saw his kids growing up to become healthy and happy adults. They took over his construction business and opened rehabilitation centers in every major city in Russia.

Of course, it was only in his imagination, but it made him happy in his heart. Even his cellmates noticed that he was in a good mood. They did not understand why he looked so happy. He was in a very bad situation and they couldn't understand how he could possibly be smiling. They thought that he'd gone crazy!

Oleg decided not to wait the full five days to let them know his decision. He had already made up his mind, and he asked his people to meet him in the assembly hall. Everybody came on time because they wanted to know what he was going to say. When he entered, everyone talked very loudly and he said to himself, "Fuck, some guys are high and some are drunk, but it's only one in the afternoon."

He greeted them and suddenly silence fell in the hall. Oleg made a long speech. He talked about his criminal career -

from a young age until today - and the merits of being a criminal. He also mentioned the significant amount of money that his group contributed to the criminal common fund. He finished his speech by saying that he wanted them to let him go from this life without any negative repercussions to him or his family. The criminal lord who was present at this meeting asked Oleg to leave the hall and wait outside while they decided what they were going to do.

Oleg knew that his destiny would be decided right then and there. He started to pray. However, it was difficult for him to find the right words. He started to think about his bright future, but he could not focus. He had a feeling of emptiness inside him. He kept thinking about all the people that he had killed, beaten, or extorted money from.

Oleg told me about a time near the beginning of his career when his boss wanted to extort money from a businessman but the guy did not want to give him anything. The boss did not want to kill him or injure him because this guy was a very smart businessman and he could bring a lot of money to the organization. So, the boss ordered Oleg to find one homeless guy, put him in a rented apartment, and feed him for a few months. Later, when he got a solid and healthy look, they gave him very nice clothing and brought him to the office of the businessman who did not want to pay. And then, in front of him and his employees, Oleg took the head off a homeless guy with a single swing of his sword.

It had been many years ago, but Oleg still remembered the innocent and trusting face of the homeless guy when he lied to him about how he was going to be given a real job. The man was so happy and thankful. The homeless man said to him that his name was Andrei and that he would never forget Oleg's help. He was going to pray all his life for Oleg's good health and fortune. He had no idea that Oleg was going to cut his head off one hour later.

So, in jail and waiting for the judgment from his yesterday friends, his heart needed to ask this homeless man for forgiveness. He imagined him sitting in front of him. Oleg got down on his knees, "Andrei, you know I am a very bad person, I did not have rights to take your life, but you know I had no choice but to do it when it was ordered, or they would have cut off my head in front of the businessman instead. Of course, I could tell you everything and we could move to another city, but they would find us anyway. Andrei, almost every night I see your face in my dreams, and in my mind I always find an excuse to blame others and not me. I know you wanted me to tell you that," Oleg almost yelled. "I know! What do you fucking want from me? Yes, I am fucking guilty, no one fucking else. That's what you wanna hear?" he said very loudly and fell on the floor face down and started to cry. "I wanted to gain respect from others," he says quietly through sobs. "Please forgive me, Andrei. I beg you, please forgive me," and he punched the floor, and he tore his hair out. He stood up again, and in a towering rage he tore the shirt off of himself. "Take my fucking life," yelled Oleg. "Take my fucking life!" and he fell again on the floor face down.

A few minutes later, he calmed down. He was feeling much better, the image of Andrei disappeared and he got a feeling that Andrei finally forgave him after so many years. He now waited for the decision with peace in his heart.

They only kept him waiting for around thirty minutes, but it was the longest half hour of Oleg's entire life. His sixth sense was telling him that it was the right time to step out of the criminal world, and not only from a moral point of view. He and everybody else knew that changes were coming in the criminal world and in the former Soviet Republics. From the late 80s until the end of the 90s, criminals were the bosses in the former Soviet Republics. At the end of the 90s the police started to take over everything. Thousands of people were going to be killed in clan wars as police took criminals' businesses and kept their money. At the time, Oleg did not know that the guys who were in the meeting hall deciding his fate were all going to be killed within a couple of years. He had no idea that all his friends from the criminal world who were dreaming about the coming changes would soon be dead.

Finally, they asked him to come back into the hall to hear their decision. He stood in the middle of the hall where everybody was sitting around in chairs. The boss told him, "Oleg, I've known you for over thirty years. I even knew your father. He was an honest policeman and that is why we respected him even though he was against us. You were like a son to me and I was planning a big future for you. However, you decided to go another direction in life, and I respect that. I'm going to let you go. You know very well that nobody can leave our world alive, but you are lucky. Today you won a lottery. Your winning ticket is life! Also, nobody is going to touch you or your family outside of prison. I am sad that I am losing you and we are all disappointed in your decision but we must respect that, as you must respect ours. So, from today on you will become a normal prisoner and won't have any of the privileges that you have had up until now. You will start working eleven hours a day like the normal prisoners do and you will eat what they eat. Everybody outside of jail is going to be informed that you are no longer with us. Now you can go.

Goodbye!"

Oleg turned around and left the room without saying one word. He was happy and sad at the same time but he didn't let anyone see his conflicting emotions. He was happy because he started a new life and sad because he had spent so much time with those people and now he was no longer a part of them. It was like losing his family all over again.

Oleg explained to me that the last three years of his sentence were the most difficult, but for the first time in his life he felt truly happy. He would never forget the day after the crime boss's decision was made. Criminals of that level do not respect any of the established prison rules. They live by their own rules. When Oleg came outside for the morning workout, everyone was so surprised to see him that they stopped doing their exercises. Everyone was watching him with big eyes.

It was a big challenge for Oleg to make this change because he had never done honest work in his entire life. He was not used to following rules, working long days every day and eating almost nothing. The prison administration had never seen a guy like Oleg make such big changes in his life by himself. His ex-friends did not talk to him anymore and normal prisoners were afraid to communicate with him, so he became lonely. The only people he talked to were the Christians that he met with every Sunday.

There was one pre-retired worker who used to work for over thirty-five years in different prisons in Russia and he hated the criminals of Oleg's level. He always said, "They are a cancer of the country and all of them should be burned alive. They follow their own rules based on violence, hatred of society, and vengeance. Those people cannot never be fixed. Their ideology is based on the principles of rejecting all rules in decent society." He hated Oleg with all his heart and thought that Oleg was going to become the next crime lord. When he saw him start working as a normal prisoner, he could hardly believe his eyes. He told his colleagues that something was up, and that the criminals must be playing a game or trying to trick them. "We have to watch them very carefully. They are planning something," he would say. Even the administration of all three jails in the city and the police outside of prisons were informed about this situation.

Everyone was on standby and ready for a war.

After the gunfight and the death of a high-ranking police officer in his condo, Oleg was kind of a celebrity in the city. Of course, the journalists heard about the changes he was making in his life and they went to the prison to meet Oleg and interview him. Oleg was very surprised when he heard from the administration about this. He did not want any publicity. The journalist asked him what exactly had happened to him? Why was he working in prison like a normal prisoner? Was it true that he left the criminal world? He confirmed everything and he said it was all true. He suspected that it seemed funny and a bit bizarre to them that he would leave the criminal world. Indeed, it was funny, and at the same time it was sad. He got the impression that society wanted him to stay with the criminals and continue to do the bad things.

Oleg did not stay the full eight years in jail. Because of his good behavior, he was released after only six and a half years behind bars. The day he left the prison, he would never forget.

He told me that in order to get out of the building he had to go through three doors and a small hallway. Then, before the exit door, a prison worker gave him his personal belongings that were on him when he was jailed a few years ago. The prison guard's job was to ask questions about what he was going to do, and every month he had to show up to check in with the police department. This usual procedure normally took ten minutes. Oleg knew it well.

He recalled the previous times when he was released from jail. A beautiful limousine and five or six luxury cars with his friends in them would be waiting for him outside the gate. One of his friends would hold a bottle of expensive French champagne. Everybody would hug him and he would sit down in the limo where half-a-dozen beautiful young girls would be waiting for him, then they would drive to the most expensive restaurant in the city. During the trip he would make love with all five girls at the same time. His friends would follow his limousine in their cars and shoot their AK-47s in the air. Police would pretend not to notice anything. At the restaurant, he would drink, eat, and fuck girls all through the day, evening and night. It was a hero's welcome home.

This day was a different story though. His wife Olga had sold all his properties and cars, and she kept only one simple condo. She had to sell everything, because she had to pay the lawyer fees, and bribes to the police to get permission to see him and make sure that the food she sent to Oleg would really arrive to him. All his money was gone.

He left the building of the prison and, with the gate still

closing behind him, he saw his wife shivering in the cold. Around her were many other people with food bags waiting for their turn to get inside and bring the items to their family members who were in jail, but Oleg and Olga only saw each other. In that moment, he was ready to rip himself to pieces for the grief he had brought to his wife. She ran towards him and he ran towards her and they wrapped arms around each other and never wanted to let go.

They stayed without moving for a few minutes. Then suddenly, she said, "Oleg, I brought you a chicken soup, I hope it is not cold." And she took from her bag a jar wrapped with many cloths and towels to keep the soup warm. She quickly unwrapped it and they drank soup together. The soup was cold but for him this soup was the warmest and the best in the world. After finishing the soup, they walked, holding hands to the bus station. After a few minutes, the old and dirty bus arrived and they were gone. At that moment, they were the happiest people in the world. All was good for them.

CHAPTER TWELVE

THE FIGHT FOR FAMILY

I wanted a happy ending like Oleg and Olga but it wasn't meant to be. Francesca and I continued to struggle in our relationship. After graduation, Francesca couldn't find a job anywhere. I told her that I was making really good money, so why didn't she help me with the paperwork, and I would pay her a salary. She did not like this idea very much. She wanted to be independent. She told me that in Quebec bad things had happened in our relationship and we needed to start over somewhere new, all the way across Canada, in British Columbia. I didn't speak a word of English and had worked so hard to build clientele that I didn't want to start from scratch again! Her English was better than her French so she promised me she would start working right away and I could take a few months to learn English, without worrying about working. Also, she said she had family in Vancouver who would help us out. My parents advised me not to go because they didn't trust her at all.

I did not research about my profession in British Columbia because the complexity of transferring my license to another province and how hard it would be to find the clients there seemed too overwhelming. I was preoccupied with keeping the family together and making my son happy. I finally accepted that I had to move to Vancouver with her. It was the only choice. I was very unhappy because I lost all residual income from the clients that I had built up over the past two years in Quebec. I had very little savings because the money I had made I had invested back into my business.

I purchased leads for life insurance, hiring an assistant to do my paperwork and a person to make cold calls for me.

When we arrived in Vancouver, I did not look for work right away because I did not know how to speak English well enough. I signed up for classes to learn English and Francesca found a job right away. Since we were both busy, my mother came to Vancouver to take care of our son. But things did not work out between me and Francesca. She and my mother did not get along. Francesca was jealous of my closeness with my mother and wanted her to go home to the Ukraine. My mother accused Francesca of stealing her clothes and throwing them away. I felt afraid of the violence I felt in the air. I had grown up with violence at home. I was worried that Francesca might become violent, and even began to imagine she was poisoning my food.

At that time, I was unemployed, didn't speak English, and was going to have to move out of an apartment where I had paid the security deposit and the monthly rent. I was providing for everyone but for the second time now, it was me who had to leave. That made no sense. Things were so bad that it was becoming dangerous. She would be violent with my mother, calling her names and turning on the lights in the middle of the night where she slept. For my safety and my mother's, I knew we had to leave. We looked around and found an inexpensive basement suite in a house nearby and my son stayed with us there half the time.

I wasn't sure how angry Francesca would be about us leaving, so we had to sneak out while she was gone. We waited until she was at work, packed up all our clothes and snuck out without her knowing. I remember my first day in the new place. After paying security deposit and first month rent, I had only fifteen-hundred dollars in my pocket for all the expenses for the rest of the month. The next month was even worse. I had to pay rent and I still did not have my insurance license yet. It took over three months to transfer my license from Quebec to British Columbia. I could barely speak any English at all, and of course, after leaving Francesca I had to stop my English course. After two weeks of English, I did not learn much and the bills kept coming in. I had to purchase a new bed for my son, a lot of blankets, plates, a frying pan, and all the essentials for cooking. I made a bed out of blankets for me and my mother because I had no money for furniture. I ended up sleeping on the floor for two more years before I could afford a real bed.

There I was, sitting in my basement room, empty in my heart and empty in my pocket. I had built a solid insurance business in Quebec, then left everything there and started my life all over again from scratch.

I cried. I felt a lot of pain in my heart, and for the first time in my life, I really did not see a way to fix my situation. I did not want to live anymore. I was tired of having to build up everything from scratch again and again. It really made me depressed but I asked myself, if something happened to me what would happen to my son? Who would make sure he was taken care of? I thought Francesca would never take care of him properly. And who would take care of my parents? I did not have any answers for my questions, so I knew at that moment that it was all up to me. I couldn't take the easy way out. I had to do whatever it took to make my life a success.

I stood up from my chair, went out from my apartment and started selling cleaning products for cars, by going door-to-door like I did in the Ukraine and Quebec. Sometimes I would just approach people on the street or at the gas station. It was so humiliating to be so broke that I had to do that. Here I was, a man with a bachelor's degree in social work, who had successful business in insurance, pushing cleaning products on the street. Oh my God! But did I have another choice? No! The biggest challenge was my poor English. When I came here, I did not speak any English at all, and I did not have time to learn it. Honestly, most of the people who purchased these products from me, bought them out of pity.

Within a few months, I finally received my insurance license. I was so happy. Now I had some options, so I decided to sell the RESP (Registered Education Savings Plan) for kids. It was much easier for me to find the clients for RESPs than for life insurance. I prospected from nine a.m. until six p.m. each day, then I had meetings with clients. At ten p.m. I arrived home, ate, then slept until four a.m. At four, I woke up and taught myself English on my computer till eight a.m. I had breakfast and left to do my door-to-door work at nine a.m.

That was my life from Monday till Thursday. Friday, Saturday and Sunday I took care of my son. During the day I did not eat or drink, so that I would not waste time looking for a washroom. It was a very long day. Many long hours of walking and talking. I felt pain in my right leg again, I was hungry, and I was always thirsty for a glass of water. The most difficult time to prospect was sunny days in the summertime. Thirst followed me all day long. A few times I almost passed out from dehydration, but I always told myself: My life is beautiful, and the future is bright!

CHAPTER THIRTEEN

THE FIGHT FOR THE LIFE

I continued to do door-to-door sales for the next few years. I hoped that my son would not be forced to do what I was doing when he grew up. There were no girls, no friends, and every day was the same for three years. In Quebec, I had a choice but here I did not have any. I could not work in BC as a social worker because my English was so bad. I could not write in English or even speak it well enough.

It was at this time that I received a call from Oleg's wife. I asked her how they were doing and she told me that Oleg had been murdered. I did not know what to say but she explained to me what happened...

She said that Oleg parked his car like always, next to his apartment building. When he was about to open the front door, someone called him. The video camera of the building showed that Oleg had a long conversation with this person and then Oleg and this person made a handshake. After the handshake, the guy took out a gun slowly and pointed at Oleg. He did not even resist. The guy said something to Oleg and then shot him twice in the stomach area. Oleg fell and never got up.

Before passing away, he used all his power to take a phone from his pocket and used it to record a video message to his family.

This is what it said: "My lovely son and darling wife, I made a lot of mistakes in my life. I was a bad person, I killed and injured many people but thank God I realized that I was wrong, and I finally became a good person. I helped many people who had the same lifestyle that I got before, and they left the criminal world because of my advice. This person who just shot me had only two choices, to kill you, my son and you, my wife Olga, or kill me. I chose for them to kill me. I was very deep in the criminal world and I knew that I would one day need to pay for leaving there. Now I am talking to you my son, please do not make the same mistake that I did many years ago when I killed those guys who killed my father. Do you see what happened to me? Prisons, violence, and now I am laying down alone on the ground in a pool of blood, and I won't see you growing up. I won't be able to see and play with your kids when they are born. Please don't be mad at the guy for killing me. He had a job to do so forgive this person and let go. The only way to protect the family is to move on and make a good life for you and your mother. I love you both! Now I have to go, I hear my parents calling me..."

His life ended in a pool of blood by the front door of his condo.

I could not make it to the funeral, but I was told there were many people from the criminal world. Thousands of criminals and addicts, some who threw syringes, guns, knives, and alcohol into his coffin showing they had quit these things. There were people who Oleg had helped get out of the crime life. He was loved and had helped so many people make their lives good again without doing crimes and going to jail. He volunteered at prisons everywhere in Russia trying to help change prisoners' lives. He fought for the rights of prisoners to have bibles in their cell when they were in solitary confinement. He organized - through the government - to have businesses get tax cuts for hiring ex-prisoners. He also wanted to create a soccer team and boxing team inside the prisons to help inmates reach positive goals, however he was killed before he could complete these final goals.

It was sad news but I knew that Oleg had expected this to happen to him someday. The life he had fought for was not meant to be.

For me, after what seemed like forever, I finally started seeing some light at the end of the tunnel in my own life. My consistent, hard work was bearing fruit. I had some new residual income coming in from existing clients and I was beginning to get a lot of referrals from them as well. The day had come when I did not need to do the door-to-door sales anymore!

Not long after that I met an insurance broker who gave me some really good advice. He said I should look for accountants or lawyers as clients. Those professionals have hundreds of clients and they know their clients need financial planning. Using the Yellow Pages and Google, I contacted all the accountants in British Columbia. I talked over the phone with more than one thousand accountants and I met personally with over three hundred of them. Only two accountants were willing to refer me to their clients for financial planning but at least it was a beginning.

After five years of living in British Columbia I was finally successful in business! I had also learned English from watching YouTube and practicing with my clients. I'd been through hell and came out as the victor. I always believed, and repeated out loud to myself every day before leaving the house, "I am successful, I am rich, I have a beautiful house, I have a beautiful car, and people are calling me every day to buy insurance from me." I had a clear view of what I wanted to happen. I didn't allow negative thinking to come into my mind. When Francesca asked me to move to another province, I had only focused on keeping the family together. Even though I did not speak the language, didn't know anybody in British Columbia and had no money, I knew in my heart that I was going to become successful. With a light heart, I had left everything behind - all of the things I had worked so hard to build - because I was certain I was going to build something even bigger. Do not be scared to try new things and take risks today, because tomorrow it may be too late!

Before, when I was young, I trained a lot to prepare myself for competition. I did everything I could to win in competitions. I thought any enjoyment was bad for me. I put myself in an unnatural cage with rules that did not make any sense. I believed that in the years after my illness I could forget about my leg and I wouldn't have any problem with it, but my mind could not let it go. I constantly built artificial obstacles that I needed to overcome.

It wasn't intentional, but I put it in my head that everything in life was difficult and that included walking. Even now, I sometimes say to myself, "Just walk. Be yourself. If there is pain in your leg, then just limp. There is nothing wrong with that. Just walk from one place to another without paying any attention to how you are walking. Everybody has their own walk. Nobody cares how you are walking."

Later, when I was done with sports, I did not put crazy rules on myself about walking, but I still did not know how to enjoy life. I saw it as a constant obstacle to overcome.

I remember I was around twenty years old and my girlfriend, when she broke up with me, I asked her why. She told me, "You complicate your life and others'. Keep it simple!" And my ex-wife told me when we broke up, "You pressure me so much I feel like I cannot breathe." I did not understand this.

It was so bad that even when I was in bed with a girl I could not relax. If the girl didn't take the initiative, I could not have sex with her. I did not realize that having sex is supposed to be about pleasure. You do not need to analyze why the people like having sex, because it is natural. I felt like a prisoner of my thoughts and my mood depended on my thinking. I tried to control everything and if it did not work as I thought it should, I became irritated and raised my voice or even yelled at them. The older I became, the more I realized that the universe had intelligence and wanted to help us. Francesca once yelled at me "You want everything to be done perfectly!" And yes, I did want everything to be perfect. For my son.

I did not understand that no parent is perfect. I had different views from Francesca about parenting. I wanted him to be eating what I thought was proper and sleeping when I thought he should! I took him out on walks two times a day even in negative forty-degree weather in Quebec. I believe the universe sent me someone who was the exact opposite of me, somebody who had very different views to me about keeping a schedule for the child, and about keeping a clean apartment and what sort of food to eat. She did not pay attention to these details in everyday life in the way I thought she should. However, I paid too much attention to details. The universe sent her to me so I would learn one important lesson, that when we focus too much on the details, we forget to be happy.

When I was walking, I wanted to walk perfectly. I wanted to have a perfect relationship. In my eyes, I thought everything must be perfect or I would not be happy. Of course, life is not perfect, it is just what I thought it could be. I had the impression that if I put limitations on everything, it would be like I was putting myself in control. That was why the universe was trying to help me, by sending people and situations that I did not like, and that contradicted my unreasonable standards. I needed reasonable problems to learn to accept life, and not the made-up problems that were in my head.

When I arrived in Vancouver, I went through hell for the first three years but I survived, and when I accepted my fate and focused on making the best of things. I even made enough money to purchase a condo. One year later, I sold this condo and made a healthy profit. I was incredibly happy that I made this profit and after that I decided to rent a nice apartment.

Everything was fine in my life. Business was good, and I started to date a beautiful girl from Brazil. I did not need to sell door to-door anymore. I started to enjoy my life and had enough referrals from existing clients to be happy with. Plus, I invested the money in segregated funds and made a good profit every month. It would seem that I should just have just sat back and enjoyed my life. I cannot explain what happened in my head, but at that time, I felt restless and started to spend time on Craigslist looking for properties or businesses to purchase.

I did not want to buy anything, but I continued to look for something, I don't know what.

One day I saw a house for sale on the river, not too far from downtown Vancouver. I really fell in love with this property, but the price was so high and the house was in very bad condition. Logic told me to not even consider buying it because I did not need it, but my heart pushed me to at least go look. One day, I drove there to see the place without setting up an appointment with the owner. As soon as I saw it, I fell even more in love with it. When I got out of my car, I just stood there, watching the house and I couldn't even move. I was standing in the parking lot listening to the lapping of the water in the river. Birds were singing and I said to myself, "This is exactly what I want."

When I was inside of this house, I was shocked at the awful condition it was in. Honestly, it was so bad that it needed to be torn down. The owner of this house was a smart guy and he saw right away how impressed I was with the location of this property. He put pressure on me, lying and telling me that he had multiple offers. I ended up paying more than the asking price. Unfortunately, I did not have an inspection done and I did not know anything about construction or renovation. The general contractor that I hired knew it and took advantage of me too. I overpaid for the renovation. To finish the repairs, I had to get a second mortgage with a private lender at a very high interest rate. Because of all this, I only lived in this house for eight months. I had to sell my beautiful place because the mortgage payments and the interest were too high.

I was under a lot of financial pressure to sell so I sold this house under the asking price. After selling my house I was in debt, badly. I had lost hundreds of thousands of dollars! Of course, I was extremely disappointed with myself for losing so much money.

But there was a funny thing. After my house was sold, I realized that I had been focusing less on my leg while walking. I felt that I let go of a little bit of baggage in my heart. It is hard to explain but I started to breathe easier after this failure with my house. I mean, when I would breathe in, it felt lighter in my heart. There was less pressure.

I was still terribly upset until one day I had a dream. In my dream I saw myself sleeping in the house that I just sold. An old man approached my bed and he bowed, basically paid homage to me, and he said, "Thank you for everything." I realized that in my dream this old man was the first owner of this house.

See, when I started the renovation - to save money as much as I could - I participated in demolishing the walls, tearing up the floors, removing all the garbage, and more. After opening the floor, I cleaned under the floorboards and I found an old picture. It was a picture of a man and his wife. I had a good relationship with my neighbors and showed them the picture. They told me that this was the couple who built the house. This was how I knew that the old man who came to me in my dreams was the first owner, and he said thank you to me for properly renovating the house.

After this dream, I analyzed this situation with my house. I finally understood that I needed to go through this difficulty because without struggling I would not be able to change my emotional problems. In the past, I always tried to be easy-going but, in this situation - when it did not work out how I planned - I was extremely negative, emotional, and even aggressive. After selling the house, something changed inside of me. I became more flexible and easy-going. I felt that it was like baggage that had fallen from my neck. But I also felt that I still had a lot of stuff to clean up and change inside myself. For example, internal programs in my subconscious - like low self-esteem and dissatisfaction with myself - were still running wild inside of me. But that also means that new adventures are waiting for me! So, I will put my face towards the wind, and yell, "Life! I am thankful for everything!"

I thought that the fight for the life had changed meaning for me many times through my experiences but now I think I have learned that it has always been a fight to find a way in life that makes you happy. I believe that it helps to open up or realize your talents, even if they are hidden very deep inside of you. In our society, work is a necessity. Especially for me. As an immigrant, I have almost no one in Canada. No one can support me financially, so I did not have any choice but to work. Meanwhile, I have my parents to support, my son to support - at least until he needs it no longer - and myself also to support. So, I work from eight to four and live from paycheck to paycheck like the majority of people in the world do.

However, I know for sure that I am still a prisoner of my mind. I still can not relax while I am walking. Yes, my leg was sick but it has been well over ten years since the illness has subsided. I still cannot let it go. Even though I am going in the right direction with work, I still have not done enough to fix my state of mind. I still cannot find the exit to the room where my mind has put me. It is basically a fight with myself. However, it now seems easier to achieve. I just need to accept myself for who I am, love myself, appreciate myself, forgive myself, live in the present moment, and be happy. My leg has been the indicator that I have not achieved harmony or friendship with myself. Hopefully one day it will happen. Until then, I will just keep repeating to myself, "Life is beautiful, and the future is bright!"

When I wrote this book, I wanted to show to people that we do not need to be perfect to do something amazing. Society wants us to be perfect at work, perfect in our personal relationships, be perfect wife or husband, father, mother, etc. But by doing that we are only imitating each other, not being ourselves. Our values and life principles seem to be based on society's opinion. When we do that, we stop being ourselves and become afraid to make mistakes in the eyes of others.

I was refusing those stereotypes.

For many years, I tried to imitate somebody else's walk to be more perfect. I wanted people to like how I was walking and instead of walking like I naturally do, I changed myself into someone else. We should be who we naturally are, not copycats of someone else.

There will always be a fight on the inside of me. I would say it is a fight of contradiction. I am always trying to live life without caring about other opinions of me but at the same time I realize that I am not going to win this fight. This world is duality, the fight between both sides.

However, at least in my book I want to be myself. I have never learned English in school. I learned English over the past five years on the street, while I was talking to everyday people. I am able to write a book with my words, and I will continue to write because I have many stories I need to share. I just want to show you the power of mind in every life through my story.

If you believe in yourself and be yourself, you will accomplish everything you ever wanted to, and you don't have to be perfect to do it.

- Urii Orlov

ABOUT THE AUTHOR

Urii Orlov grew up in Odessa, Ukraine where life was rough and times were harder. He learned at an early age to fight for what he needed and take what he could to survive.

The Ukraine is rife with gangs and mafia, which offers a life of luxury to starving young boys. Urii spent time learning how to survive in some of the roughest areas in the city. He learned to be tougher than the toughest, while battling health challenges and a violent family environment. Through it all he felt a calling to be a better person and leave the life of violence and crime for a life of service.

He is a natural learner and used his intelligence to pull himself off the streets and into university where he completed his degree in Social Work. His desire to help others led him to healthcare services and then to financial planning services all in an effort to help others better their own lives.

His many unusual life experiences have led him to share his metaphysical discoveries, and to help others unwind the mysteries of their own life. By sharing his and others' strange adventures, he hopes to give his readers an insight into how life works so they can learn from his experiences and focus on what they want to achieve in their own life. His positive attitude inspires hope and makes achieving goals and dreams seem possible.

Urii currently resides in Maple Ridge, BC, and has begun working on his next book.

Canadian Allied Services, 2022

Made in the USA
Columbia, SC
26 January 2023

10267329R00074